Pathfinders for Christianity in Northern Nigeria (1862–1940)

"With assiduous scholarly research, diligent data analysis, and refreshing critical candor, Emmanuel Egbunu does commendable justice to the lives and work of his predecessors in the service of God's church not only in Northern Nigeria but throughout the country. May God use this testimony to the work of faith and labor of love of the pioneers to equip his church with patience, endurance, and hope in facing the battles of the present and the future."

—EMMANUEL OLADIPO,
Retired Director, Scripture Union International

"In this excellent historical account of the work of CMS in the Lokoja area in Nigeria between 1862 and 1941, Egbunu shows us exactly why African Christians need to write histories of their own communities. He rightly shines the light on parts of the story that could only be best told by Africans, saving them from being forever lost. Through his hard work of research and writing, he models for us the role of ecclesial leaders as both researchers and storytellers. Anyone interested in the history of Christianity in Africa, especially during the colonial era, will find this book helpful. I cannot recommend it highly enough."

—HARVEY KWIYANI,
Lecturer, Liverpool Hope University

"This captivating study significantly extends our insight into the pioneering role of the Nigerian agents of CMS Anglican Church in the introduction of Christianity and Western education to Northern Nigeria, especially during the heyday of colonialism. Drawing on archival, oral, and secondary sources, Bishop Egbunu analyzes the dynamics of the mission practices and experiences of the indigenous pathfinders of Christianity at the Niger-Benue Confluence and the enduring impact of their exertions."

—FEMI KOLAPO,
Professor of African History, University of Guelph

"The life, ministry, and impact of the legendary Bishop Samuel Ajayi Crowther will for a long time continue to attract the attention of scholars, ministers, historians, linguists, and all shades of inquiring minds. Crowther remains the role model par excellence for genuine missionaries and nationalists in Africa. . . . Egbunu's use of language in this book is lucid and simple, yet it reflects stylistic erudition and analytical depth. . . . In an age of advanced secular culture, communism, liberal theology, biblical revisionism, church decline, and radical redefinition of evangelism and how to do missions, retelling the life story of Bishop Samuel Crowther is most significant as a tonic to reinvigorate the church's return to Christian orthodoxy and rekindle the fire of missions again, to all nations of the world."

—DAPO F. ASAJU,
Professor of Theology, Lagos State University

Pathfinders for Christianity in Northern Nigeria (1862–1940)

Early CMS Activities at the Niger-Benue Confluence

EMMANUEL A. S. EGBUNU

Foreword by G. O. M. Tasie

RESOURCE *Publications* • Eugene, Oregon

PATHFINDERS FOR CHRISTIANITY IN NORTHERN NIGERIA
(1862–1940)
Early CMS Activities at the Niger-Benue Confluence

Resource Publications
An Imprint of Wipf and Stock Publishers
199 W. 8th Ave., Suite 3
Eugene, OR 97401

www.wipfandstock.com

PAPERBACK ISBN: 978-1-6667-0637-6
HARDCOVER ISBN: 978-1-6667-0638-3
EBOOK ISBN: 978-1-6667-0639-0

DECEMBER 28, 2021

For 'Biodun

With unceasing admiration, affection, and appreciation

Contents

List of Images

FOREWORD

WE WELCOME YET ANOTHER CONTRIBUTION to the ever-mounting body of literature in Nigerian Christian history. And significantly, this work is an addition by Dr. Emmanuel Egbunu, the pioneer Archbishop of the Lokoja Ecclesiastical Province of the Church of Nigeria (Anglican Communion).

This addition is, in very many dimensions, the new extension of our knowledge of the legendary Bishop Samuel Ajayi Crowther; especially the hitherto-untold history of Bishop Crowther's missionary work among the various peoples of the Niger-Benue confluence region. The work also shows how, despite Crowther's travails in the well-known Niger Mission crises of the 1880s, he was still able to open the way for Christian missionary work and initiate varied significant influence in parts of Nigeria, north of the Niger-Benue Rivers. Significantly, Dr. Egbunu has demonstrated how, if only Bishop Crowther's carefully thought-out templates for cordial interreligious relationships (especially among Christian and Muslim adherents) had been heeded, the ugly interreligious disharmony, as we notice in Nigeria today, could have been much minimized in favor of better understanding and cooperation.

The author has made highly remarkable, good use of the location of his ecclesiastical seat in Lokoja: the one-time big commercial center and administrative hub of Colonial Nigeria, as well as the beehive of missionary work (especially of the Church Missionary Society, or CMS). He has also used this opportunity to revisit and utilize available source materials—some of them invaluable human and material sources, hitherto not utilized (as far as I know) by other researchers. Equally remarkable is his superb knowledge of as many secondary sources as, I believe, he could (humanly speaking) identify and access. Besides, he offers some new interpretations to suggest that indeed scholarship is an unending business!

I highly commend Archbishop Dr. Emmanuel Egbunu's industry, clear scholarly eyes, and diligence, especially since he has been able to do so much, in addition to his also highly demanding ecclesiastical responsibilities. This is indeed a very interesting work, written in lucid English, which was Dr. Egbunu's initial academic discipline before he migrated to Church History.

Sir Professor G.O.M. Tasie, FNAL, OFR
Former Professor of Church History, University of Jos, Nigeria

PREFACE

THE MOTIVATION AND PURPOSE OF this research was to reconstruct the legacy of the Church Missionary Society (CMS), both Western and African, in the Lokoja Niger-Benue Confluence area, with the objective of laying emphasis on the impact of the legacy on the church in Nigeria and non-Christian communities in the Niger-Benue confluence. The historic town of Lokoja enjoys the pride of place as the first British settlement in Nigeria outside the colony of Lagos. All the phases of encounter with foreign influences—commercial, missionary, and colonial—were fully experienced here as well. The Lander brothers had already found the Niger-Benue confluence by October 1830, while the Niger expeditions of 1841, 1854, and 1857 all recorded major activities around the same confluence of the two rivers Niger and Benue (then called Kworra and Tshadda, respectively).

The task of historical reconstruction throws up a range of perspectives and various interpretations about people and events which are the staple concerns of historiography. For a setting that has been more than the apparent confluence of two rivers, the Lokoja Niger-Benue Confluence area, with its multiplicity of peoples, cultures, religions, and external influences, was a natural hotbed of inevitable contention, rivalry, and turbulence.

We may ask: What was the timeline of encounters in the Niger-Benue confluence area like? After the adventurous feat of the Lander brothers, who had passed the confluence in October 1830, the area became notorious as a slave trading region—a situation which fueled the intertribal conflicts even after the evil trade had been outlawed by the British Parliament. There were wars between the powerful rival kingdoms of the Nupe and the Igala, and in the local communities there was banditry. The same area encountered explorers and merchants who sought to introduce as substitutes to the trade in slaves, legitimate trade, the Bible, and the plough. The missionaries keyed into these opportunities through the trailblazing efforts of the Church Missionary Society (CMS) in 1857, followed by the Society of African Missions (SMA) of the Roman Catholic Church in 1884, and the Cambridge Universities Missionary Party (CUMP), followed still by the influence of the first wave of indigenous expressions of Christianity—the *Aladura* revival of the 1930s. The colonial administrators took their turn in the later decades that brought in the scramble for Africa, or partition of Africa, by European nations at the Berlin conference in 1884. There were schools, health care facilities, model farms, companies, and there was criminality. In a nutshell, there was the good, the bad, the ugly.

This historical reconstruction necessitated extensive archival research which was carried out in the National Archive in Kaduna, the CMS Archive in the Cadbury's Collection of the University of Birmingham, the University of Liverpool Library, and the Andrew Walls Center for the Study of African and Asian Christianity in the Liverpool Hope University, all in the United Kingdom. Libraries and online resources were accessed and surviving individuals who benefited from CMS activities in the confluence area were interviewed. The research came up with major findings such as the surviving landmarks of missionary activities on the Niger-Benue Confluence Area; Gbobe, where the first baptism in Northern Nigeria was officiated. A significant conclusion of this research is how the solid foundation of respectful and peaceful dialogue laid by Bishop Samuel Ajayi Crowther has impacted positively on the relationship between Christians and Muslims in Lokoja metropolis for decades. It is hoped that the Lokoja model of relative peaceful coexistence between Christians and Muslims be adopted by other communities made up of similar religious adherents in Nigeria as a tested and trusted guarantee for social stability.

The Lokoja Niger-Benue confluence area also lies in the intersection between the bustling southern regions of Abeokuta, Onitsha, Bonny, Aboh, and Akoko, which were key locations of missionary encounter, and the vast North, which was then dominated by Islam and traditional religion. This range of influences therefore made crisis inevitable, whether sooner or later. Charting a pathway for Christianity in such an atmosphere was a feat of courage, determination, and perseverance. The story cannot be told all at once, or, indeed, from one perspective. Ever unfolding facets in historiography are therefore inevitable in tracing the landmarks and legacies of such a momentous encounter.

ACKNOWLEDGMENTS

To God alone be the glory and thanksgiving for bringing this work to the stage of being available to a wider audience beyond the limited postgraduate school for which this was initially undertaken as my doctoral research. It was primarily to equip me to offer my very best in God's service by getting a more detailed knowledge of the antecedents of Christian missions in the historic town of Lokoja and its surrounding area, where stories circulate with much nostalgia about the heritage of the missionaries and the legacies. The area is now the setting of my episcopal jurisdiction.

I am thankful to Professor Godwin O. M. Tasie, who, after supervising my dissertation for a Masters degree in West African Church History, encouraged me to go further. This work was begun under his meticulous guidance, but as relocations, distance, and increased ministry responsibilities stalled the progress of this work, Professor Musa A. B. Gaiya—also mentored by Professor Tasie—encouraged my renewed determination, giving every possible encouragement and taking up the supervision with unforgettable commitment. Thanks to Professor Shaibu A. Owoeye of Obafemi Awolowo University, my external examiner, who withheld his smile until the defence was over!

I must mention the untiring prodding of a good number of friends and teachers, such as the Rt. Rev. (Professor) Emmanuel B. Ajulo and his wife, Mrs Victoria A. Ajulo; Professor Danny McCain; Professor Imo Cyril; Professor Pic Onwuchei; Professor

Jotham M. Kangdim; Professor Pauline M. Lere, Professor Yoilah
Yilpet, Professor Victor Adetula; and Professor Timothy Oyetunde.

Away from my immediate setting, I am much indebted to
Professor Andrew Walls, who, as visiting professor to the University of Jos, offered attention and trusted guidance, and with
Professor Daniel Jeyaraj, Director of the Andrew Walls Centre
for the Study of African and Asian Christianity at the Liverpool
Hope University in the UK, invited me to Summer conferences
and welcomed me into postgraduate Summer classes with gener-
ous assistance; and thanks to my dear colleague and friend, Dr.
Sara Fretheim—also from the Liverpool Hope connection—who
has remained an unrelenting encourager in this and related tasks.
I cannot easily forget the steady encouragement from Professor
Femi Kolapo of the University of Guelph in Canada, who has himself done extensive work on the same area of research and beyond,
and guided me into relevant material. The staff at the Cadbury
Special Collections of the University of Birmingham, which holds
the CMS archives, was very helpful during my visits. I am similarly
thankful to the staff of the National Archives, Kaduna. I appreciate very much the grant from Whitelands College Guild Trustees,
University of Roehampton, in actualizing this stage of the work.
Venerable Dallimore Odigie, Mr Mike Lawal, and Rev. Vincent
N. Egbunu, my older brother, who showed appreciable interest
in this historical documentation. I recall the earlier insights of my
late parents, Canon Robert and Mrs Christiana Egbunu, which
got me interested in probing into the facts about their times. My
chaplains during the period of research—Canon Victor Okporu,
Canon Julius Egbeja, and Canon Bernard Metseru—as well as my
secretary, Juliana, displayed a high sense of duty to make dead-
lines achievable. The photos are from the Diocese of Lokoja Media
Library.

My dear wife, 'Biodun has again, as always, been a great support by urging me to complete what she always believed I could
accomplish, despite the many hurdles that tempted me to abandon
the project and move on to other things. Her prayer support and
that of the children, CinwonSoko, CincinSoko, and TunciSoko,

spurred me on. One friend who kept looking forward to the completion of this work was Architect (Mrs) Lolo Ngozi Alassan. It pleased God to take her home as a martyr on 7th April 2015 while on a missionary assignment with others in the vicinity of this study. May her soul rest in peace.

List of Abbreviations

BCP	Book of Common Prayer
BM	The Basel Mission
BMS	The Baptist Missionary Society
CMS	Church Missionary Society
CUMP	Cambridge Universities Missionary Party
HRH	His Royal Highness
LMS	The London Missionary Society
MMS	The Methodist Missionary Society
NKJV	New King James Version
OFM	The Order of Friars Minor (also called Franciscans)
RCM	Roman Catholic Mission
RNC	The Royal Niger Company
SIM	Sudan Interior Mission
SMA	Society of African Missions
SPG	Society for the Propagation of the Gospel
SUM	Sudan United Mission
UMS	United Missionary Society

Chapter 1

LOKOJA *and the* NIGER-BENUE CONFLUENCE AREA

THE FIRST INHABITANTS OF THE historic town of Lokoja settled on the plateau at the top of Mount Patti[1] from about 1811. They were the Nupe of the middle belt who migrated from Gbara in Nupe land in 1759. Their first stop was Bunu in Kabba area before coming to the said plateau overlooking the present city of Lokoja when it was only a small settlement. Within three decades, initial foreign encounters had begun when the Lander brothers passed by the Niger-Benue Confluence on Monday 25th October 1830.

---

1. Variously called Mount Stirling, Mount Patteh, Mount Lokoja, Pati Lukongi (mountain of doves). See Right Rev. Bishop Crowther, *Notes on the River Niger*, Proceedings of the Royal Geographical Society of London, 1876 – 1877, Vol. 21, No. 6, pp481-498: "When I made the ascent of the river, in 1854, with Dr. Baikie, we together ascended the hill, called Mount Patteh, opposite the confluence. I cannot do better than use Dr. Baikie's words to describe the scene we saw: "From an elevation of 400 feet we saw immediately beneath us the pretty green-topped Mount Stirling; on our left was a deep ravine separating us from another flat- crowned hill; . . ." The Navy Records Society describes it further: "Along the banks numerous villages could be discerned. Far as the eye could reach, for miles and miles, the ground teemed with the exuberant vegetation. . . . The natives fancy there is a difference in the colour of the two streams, and call the Quorra the white water, while the Binue is known as the black water": *The Naval Miscellany, Vol. VII*, Susan Rose (ed).

Whatever perspective one chooses—be it commercial, missionary, or colonial—the history of foreign incursion into what now defines the geographical confines and political entity known as Nigeria highlights Lokoja, with its surrounding communities in the Niger-Benue Confluence area, as frontline locations. Indeed, Lokoja rightly claims the status of being the cradle of Christianity in Northern Nigeria and combines the subsequent historical landmarks of the colonial administration and the milestones of the political history of Nigeria, to give it a pride of place from where many other accounts take their bearing.

The first voyage to establish a settlement at the confluence was sponsored by the Liverpool merchant Macgregor Laird. It was primarily a commercial venture and set sail from Liverpool on 19th July 1832. It was a difficult journey and Pedraza records Laird's feelings:

> But throughout these exacting days Laird never lost sight of the main purpose of the expedition, which was trade. The prospect so far appeared abysmal . . . Here at the Confluence, although he could count seven large villages from the deck of the Quorra and saw the canoes passing to and fro continuously, it was with the greatest difficulty that they could get the natives interested in their trade, although otherwise they were friendly enough. Lander's stories of ivory and indigo in abundance were seen to be sadly optimistic and must have caused Laird, who had staked so much on this expedition, not a little concern.[2]

However, it was the 1841 expedition, led by Captain H.D. Trotter, which made contact with the area again. This time it was called The Philanthropic Experiment, mainly sponsored by the Society for the Extinction of the Slave Trade formed by Sir Thomas Fowell Buxton. The main objective of that expedition was to get in touch with the kings of the interior and make treaties with them to abolish slavery in exchange for regular supply of British merchandise in exchange for the produce of the country. Young Samuel Ajayi Crowther, then a catechist, was on the team as an interpreter.

2. Pedraza, *Story of Lokoja*, 14.

Two more expeditions exposed the Lokoja Niger-Benue Confluence area to foreign influence—in 1854 and 1857–64—both led by Dr William Balfour Baikie. This became the reason for the more permanent attention to Lokoja which was founded as a base for the abolition of slave trade and the conversion of those so freed.

In its present location, it is situated along the valley between Mount Patti and the confluence of the Niger-Benue rivers. It also became the rallying point for neighboring ethnic groups such as the Oworo, Igala Nupe, Bassa-Nge, Kakanda, Igbira-Koto, Bunu, and Yagba, as well as a sprinkling of Hausa settlers who arrived in such neighboring communities as Panda and Koton-Kar: around 1860. As is to be expected, the tussle between some of the claimants to the traditional chieftaincy stool has given rise to a number of versions of historical reconstructions by ethnic groups that want to legitimize their claims to ownership of Lokoja. However, the account by Howard J. Pedraza, and the journals of the explorers and missionaries who had no such sentiments, are more objective. The Niger-Benue Confluence area covered in this study includes the Lokoja, Bassa country to the East of Lokoja, the Oworo to the North, and the Igbira, Kakanda, and Panda settlements to the northeast of Lokoja.

The Niger-Benue Confluence Areas in the Larger Christian History in Nigeria

Compared with the plethora of historical accounts about the beginnings of a more sustained missionary encounter (otherwise known as the replanting of Christianity in 1842, in view of earlier efforts), a major gap exists by way of detailed accounts of missionary activities in this area, especially after the death of Bishop Ajayi Crowther. Concerning the earlier Christian encounter, Ayandele notes:

> As early as 1471 Pope Sixtus IV had assigned the Christianization of the Atlantic seaboard of West Arica to the Archbishop of Lisbon. In the 17th Century, Domingos I, an Itsekiri prince educated in Portugal encouraged the

spread of Christianity when he ascended the throne, and one Aglongo, king of Dahomey (1789–1797), embraced Christianity as introduced by Portuguese missionaries.[3]

Other references are made to these earlier efforts by other scholars.[4] Tasie refers to those earlier efforts as some "lesser ripples" in Northern Nigeria in 1688 in Agadez, north of Kano by the Belgian Franciscan Brother Peter Farde, OFM, who introduced Christianity to his master. These scholars also record the efforts of the Spanish Capuchin and Italian Capuchin missions to Benin and Warri in the sixteenth and seventeenth centuries.

The timeline of Christian missionary engagement in the Niger-Benue Confluence may be traced more accurately when viewed against the larger context of early Christian missionary engagement in Nigeria. Already some phases of Christian encounter within the larger context of Nigeria have been suggested by notable scholars. For instance, Ade-Ajayi delineates the period covered by his monumental study (1841–1891) as the first phase which he termed the seedling time preparatory to the more intricate period of British colonial rule. This first phase is marked by the first Niger Expedition at the beginning, and the death of Bishop Samuel Ajayi Crowther at the end. Tasie, whose major work, *Christian Missionary Enterprise in the Niger Delta,* covering 1864–1918, has, in a more recent work—an inaugural lecture titled "The Vernacular Church and Nigerian Christianity"—presented a map of missionary engagement under the following categorization:

> The *Foreign Origin Phase,* beginning from the early nineteenth-century missionary endeavors in the 1840s to about 1914 . . . The *Response Phase* with its inclinations towards self-actualization in vernacularism up to the late 1960s, but overlapping with our first phase from about 1906 . . . The *enigmatic Church Boom Phase,* from the late 1960s, still unfolding in its tendencies.[5]

---

3. Ayandele, *Historical Studies,* 56

4. Makozi and Afolabi, *History of the Catholic Church in Nigeria.*

5. Tasie, "Vernacular Church," 2 (italics original).

This study focuses on the next stage of missionary activities in the Lokoja Niger-Benue Confluence area from the time of Bishop Crowther's death in 1891 to the time of the first centenary of the replanting of Christianity in Nigeria, being 1941. This fifty-year period, being the second half of the missionary presence, poses the challenge to establish whether or not Christianity had been firmly rooted as a credible faith and embraced by the indigenous community. This period also falls within the larger period of what Tasie calls the response stage and a gradual transition from foreign to native leadership as envisaged by the missionary statesman, Henry Venn, the friend of Africa, despite the odds and hiccups in the process.

By this time, Christianity had been planted, and a distinct group of adherents of various descriptions could be identified, ranging from commercially motivated adherents to those of low social rank who were often the ready firstfruits both in apostle Paul's missionary experience in the early stages of Christianity, and in contemporary mission enterprise. For instance, apostle Paul wrote to the young believers in Corinth: "Brothers, think of what you were when you were called. Not many of you were wise by human standards; not many were influential; not many were of noble birth" (1 Cor 1:26).

Since baptism is generally accepted as the initiatory Christian rite, the list of the firstfruits of the mission—the first baptized candidates in Gbobe, which was the first CMS station not only at the confluence, but in the entirety of northern Nigeria—must be our definite starting point. Ajayi Crowther's record of this great beginning is reproduced in Appendix A, for it shows more than just the names.

For these converts to have offered themselves for baptism in those days was a bold step, given the context of hostility. It was, for them, like literally laying down their lives to be exposed to ostracism from their families and neighbors, for they were considered by some as renegades who had denied the religion of their ancestors, or even Islamic religion, which was the earlier alternative. Some of the persecutions encountered are alluded to in later chapters of this work. Yet the Christian faith became firmly rooted through the decades and came to be owned by both natives and settlers. Since most records of the first baptism on 14th September 1862, conducted by Ajayi Crowther himself, put the figure of candidates at eight adults and one infant, it is plausible to assume that more than one baptism took place that year and this completes the entire list, arranged according to tribal affinity, rather than the sequence of dates or the exact number baptized on one occasion. Indeed, all he wrote at the end of this list was, "List of baptized Candidates at Gbebe—1862."[6]

It is noteworthy that during the period following Crowther's death—about three decades after this exciting beginning—church and other historians focused more attention on rising nationalistic movements. The most frequent issues were related to the widespread dissatisfaction with missionary Christianity that had become scandalized by instances of racial undertones. The record of the legacies of the missionaries in shaping the religious and socioeconomic life of the people did not take into proper account the peculiarities of ministry in the Lokoja Niger-Benue Confluence area, where indeed multiple factors were at play. The impressions about Christian missionary methods at the time were that they were an attempt to transplant, verbatim, the modes of worship of the mother churches of the West, and indeed to pass on the hostilities that had resulted in denominational factions even when the same historical circumstances were not replicated here. So, in addition to the intertribal conflicts of the traditional African setting and the jihadist military campaigns that sold their captives into slavery, denominational factions also became part of the scenario. This was not as pronounced in the Niger-Benue Confluence area in the earlier decades of the replanting of Christianity as they came to be in the early decades of the twentieth century.

This book is aimed at filling the gap created by the absence of historical attention to the progress of missionary Christianity in the Niger-Benue Confluence area, following the Niger Mission crisis and the subsequent demise of Bishop Crowther in 1891.

6. CA3/04/118.

It is important to establish how the missionary enterprise commenced by the CMS continued to advance with a distinct agenda that set the missionaries apart from the traders and colonialists in the Lokoja Niger-Benue Confluence area. The takeover of mission schools which had been a major legacy of missionary education had severe consequences—a development which brought considerable setback in the development and enlightenment of the research area. That notwithstanding, the most enduring landmark of the missionary encounter—both for Christian converts and adherents of other religious beliefs within the communities—was the provision of Western education, with a strong emphasis on character formation and societal cohesion. This eventually became the foundation for a stable society with healthy interrelationships between varying faiths and cultural divides.

The Niger-Benue Confluence Area at the Turn of the Twentieth Century

At the beginning of the period from 1891 to 1941, Bishop Crowther had just died under unsavory circumstances in the CMS mission, and his ministry landmarks were solidly on ground in the Lokoja Niger-Benue Confluence area. The Holy Trinity Church and School, which he had established in 1865, still stood, and the enrollment in both cases continued to grow gradually as a service to the entire community. It is noteworthy that the register of pupils at the school included more than just Christians. Even the nobility from other religions had released their wards to receive Western education at the school. The reigning traditional ruler in Lokoja at the time of this study, HRH Alhaji Mohammadu Kabir Maikarfi III, is a product of the school. He personally testifies that he was even a chorister but was not compelled to convert. His posture has doused tensions repeatedly in the face of rising religious tensions by bigoted religious adherents.

Lokoja became the focus of landmark political events that formed the cradle of the Nigerian nation, especially with the appointment of Sir Frederick Lugard as Governor General by the

British Government on January 1, 1900. Other notable events were soon to follow, including the amalgamation in 1914 of the Northern and Southern protectorates, as well as the hoisting of the Royal Niger Company flag.

Another significant feature of Christianity in the Niger-Benue Confluence area at this time, and specifically in the 1930s, was the emergence of strands of African independent churches, with their strong emphasis on prophetic and miraculous manifestations. A further dimension to missionary Christianity beyond the emphasis on commercial interests of the early days was in the area of education and medical missions, which flourished in the mission stations around the confluence during this period, drawing patriots from the neighboring tribes of Nupe, Oworo, Igala, and indeed Igbirra to the schools established at Kpata and Akabe. Early in the period covered by this research (1891–1941), a number of native expressions of Christianity had begun to spring up in the form of revival movements within the political entity now known in Nigeria (and indeed much of Africa) to address some pertinent spirituality gaps in the mission churches. The first of these, though far away in the Bonny area, was the *Teke* prayer movement by Garrick Sokari Braide from about 1912–1915. Closely following this was the Faith Tabernacle movements around 1918, which were championed by J. B. Sadare and a few others from St. Savior's Anglican Church in Ijebu-Ode. Sophia Odunlami, a schoolteacher, soon joined the society which was then called Precious Stone Society (later called Diamond Society). Their distinctive practices were their belief in divine healing, baptism of the Holy Spirit, personal holiness, rejection of infant baptism, and the premillennial return of Christ.

From the 1930s the wave of the *Aladura* brand of the Independent Church movement had spread its influence very strongly over the Niger-Benue Confluence area so that many people made long journeys to some of the revival centers where they witnessed the power of God at work in a way that was unknown within the CMS brand of Christianity. Akin Omoyajowo identifies these independent churches as: "those indigenous churches which began to emerge in Nigeria from the second decade of this century [20th century]. . . . They are churches which began as indigenous churches, founded by indigenous persons and run under indigenous leadership."[7]

A point of interest in the Lokoja Niger-Benue Confluence area which has not enjoyed the attention of church historiographers is in the area of important institutions that were introduced by the CMS within the first three decades of the twentieth century. They include a school for the training of catechists and evangelists, located at Amewa at the bank of the River Niger further east of the confluence. A number of those trained there became the evangelists and pastors both for the area—especially the Bassa and Oworo lands—and even further afield to Nupe land in present-day Niger State. It is significant that while Islam in Nupe land pursued a military expansionist and colonizing agenda towards the confluence, Christian missions actually reached out with the gospel from the confluence to Nupe land and indeed the first Nupe evangelists came from the Bassa community of the Niger-Benue Confluence area.

Besides the mission stations at Kpata, Lokoja, Kippo Hill, and Egga, other CMS institutions at this time included a boarding house which was a kind of convent for young girls under the tutelage and supervision of the CMS missionary Miss Catherine Matthew. There was also the earlier mentioned elementary school and the maternity home, both at Akabe, with hostels for young boys and girls who were under the nurture of the CMS missionary there, Miss K. E. Ritsert. Akabe town became a Christian community with a church, school, maternity, and boarding house equipped with water storage facilities.

Of further relevance is the fact of conflicting cultural worldviews as the Christian converts struggled with the imperialistic trappings and colonial excesses of missionary Christianity. These vestiges of colonialism further fueled the nationalistic sentiments that gave birth to the Independent African Churches. There was a need to interpret Christianity within the native worldview lest

---

7. Omoyajowo, "Aladura Churches in Nigeria," 96.

adherents should become native strangers by simply submitting to this new faith without prejudice. These concerns always haunted even scholars of African Christianity. Ayandele, in *African Historical Studies,* observed that four basic challenges confronted the African Church, namely,

> how the transplanted churches from Europe and the New World are to be transformed into the Church of God in which African cultures can integrate, in which the African can worship uninhibited emotionally or psychologically 'in spirit and in truth' . . . how institutionalized Christianity in Africa is to acquire an identity and self-dignity of its own as a unit within the organic whole of the Church Universal.[8]

Given the polyglot profile of the Lokoja Niger-Benue Confluence area, these concerns were certainly pertinent at that time.

Relocation from Gbobe to Lokoja

Gbobe had the privilege of being the first mission station, in addition to attracting the first institutions, but soon lost that status for a number of reasons. Given that the entire confluence area was sandwiched between powerful enemies such as the Nupe and the Igala between 1859 and 1860, it became volatile as the hotbed of intertribal conflicts in the community. Then came an eight-month war between some Bassa neighbors of Gbobe in 1862–1863. While other battles put Gbobe in a state of constant insecurity, the downturn came in January 1865 when there were six warring camps around the town. The Nupe Etsu, Massaba, launched a campaign against Gbobe, though he allowed the missionaries to evacuate.

The outbreak of civil war in Gbobe, which included a clash of contestants to the throne, resulted in the destruction of the town, including the mission structures. Consequently, the mission station relocated to Lokoja on the opposite side of the confluence in

---

8. Ayandele, *African Historical Studies,* 107.

1865. It was in Lokoja that same year that the Holy Trinity Church and School were later established by Bishop Ajayi Crowther.

It is apparent that the Niger-Benue Confluence had an established pattern of community life dominated by much economic and religious activity in the form of slave trade, and the advance of Islam, with its military expansionist tendency. However, the impact of each of these strands of influences can be analyzed only in terms of the enduring social structures and value systems that have now emerged from these encounters.

It would be unwieldy to attempt to string together the various facets of missionary impact as recorded by historiographers with different concerns, biases, and perspectives. While some, like J. F. Ade-Ajayi, William Olaseinde Ajayi, and Modupe Oduyoye, have devoted attention in various ways to the advent of missions in the more sustained effort of the replanting of Christianity in 1842 by the Methodists and the Church Missionary Society (CMS), others like Emmanuel A. Ayandele, Michael Crowder, and Godwin Tasie have sought to evaluate and analyze the political and sociocultural impact of this encounter between the foreign and the indigenous. Conflicts are inevitable in such encounters, and in most cases, it was clearly a conflict of worldviews, mostly cultural and religious. This observation is corroborated by A. F. Walls in a CMS interview in their *Yes* magazine, as he speaks about Ajayi Crowther's impact:

> Here is one of Africa's first great modern (Christian) leaders. For us today he is able to liberate Christianity from its association with colonialism, revealing it to be a worldly force able to undo the evil of slavery and rebuild society according to spiritual principles. He proves that everything you were told about the missionaries and the empire is wrong. . . . By 1875, the colonial era was beginning and within 16 years Crowther had died a broken man, his work abandoned and buried. His superiors appointed a European in his place, believing that Africans lacked the capacity to rule. The Yoruba turned to nationalism and sectarianism in response.[9]

9. Walls, in Sturdy, "Do Not Despise," 9.

This situation continued as long as the African story was told from the perspective of foreigners, which were characteristically tainted by fundamental prejudices. What the missionaries of this period regarded as conversions were often influenced by multiple interests which were not always pure, prominent among them being the hope for military and commercial benefits. Individual conversions were not emphasized, and the assumption was that the declared assent of the traditional ruler was tantamount to the conversion of the subjects, the long-term implication being a faith that was, at best, superficial, and which therefore balked in the face of crisis.

E. O. Babalola's book, *Christianity in West Africa: The Historical Analysis,* covers the beginning of the replanting of Christianity in West Africa in places like Sierra Leone, Liberia, Gold Coast (Ghana), The Gambia, and Nigeria. He also provides an overview of the phases and varieties of Christian presence in West Africa, noting the factors for their successes and failures. A number of missionary agencies were involved: The CMS, the Basel Mission, the Society for the Propagation of the Gospel, The Methodist Missionary Society, and the Baptist Missionary Society. The London Missionary Society, founded in 1795, also inspired the other evangelical groups among the Anglicans, Methodists, and Scottish Presbyterians as the fruit of the Evangelical Revival of early-nineteenth-century England. The Roman Catholic Church also had its own societies for the same purpose. They include The Society of the African Mission, the Holy Ghost Fathers, and the White Fathers.

Babalola records a number of historical landmarks from this time: the arrival of the first English-speaking Christian missionary in Badagry in September 1842 the first Christian baptism, which took place in Abeokuta (including Ajayi Crowther's aged mother) in 1848; the confirmation of 500 people; the ordination of two Yoruba men to the order of deacon during the visit of Bishop Vidal of Sierra Leone to Nigeria in 1854; and the move by Samuel Ajayi Crowther, accompanied by Rev. John Christopher Taylor, to Onitsha, which became the first station of the Niger Mission. In all these events, there is only a brief mention of the elaborate work done in the Lokoja Confluence area, which became the gateway of Christianity to the North: "The party succeeded in penetrating the hinterland as far as Nupe country but with losses of their boats and personal effects. The members of the expedition remained at Rabah for a long time because it was a convenient meeting place for the Yoruba and Hausa people."[10]

By the turn of the century, the Lokoja Confluence area was no longer a big interest for historiographers, whose attention had shifted to other climes. However, Babalola states that:

> By 1902, Dr Walter Miller of the CMS Pioneer party had returned to Girku with the government's approval. In 1903, the CMS was permitted to operate at Bida and in the Bussa country and by 1914 they had five stations. At Bida in the Nupe country they even founded a school where both Nupe and Hausa were taught in the European alphabet. In 1905, the mission headquarters was transferred to Zaria at the invitation of the Emir. Though some few converts were baptized in Zaria in 1907 and at Bida in 1912, there were restrictions on public preachings [sic] or worship in these towns and these had to be conducted in private houses. In 1907, an extension of missionary work among the Animist tribes began, this time on Bauchi Plateau when the Cambridge University Party whose object was to work among Mohammedans and ethno religionists whom they called Animists opened their stations here.[11]

10. Babalola, *Christianity in West Africa*, 93.
11. Babalola, *Christianity in West Africa*, 96.

Gbobe Chapel at the site of the first Baptism in northern Nigeria,
14th September 1862

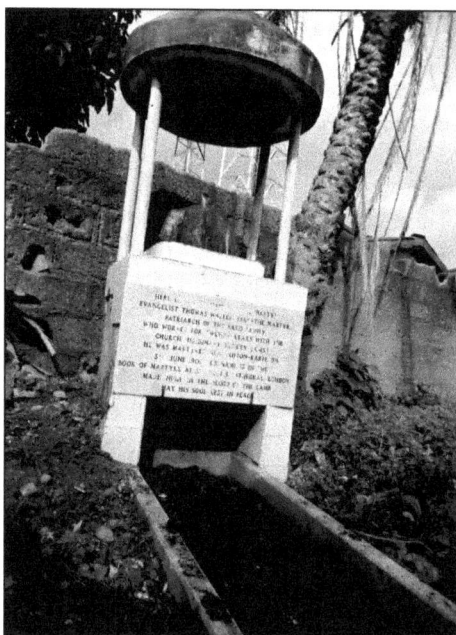

Lokoja: The grave of Evangelist Thomas Walter Bako, the martyr.

Chapter 2

A HISTORICAL SURVEY *of the* TERRAIN OF CMS ENGAGEMENT

LOKOJA, WHICH AT A POINT was called Lairdstown in honor of MacGregor Laird (the younger son of the famous firm of Liverpool shipbuilders), began as a commercial city. As early as the first expedition up the River Niger in 1832, of which MacGregor Laird was both originator and a driving spirit, specific mention had been made of the location which was to become Lokoja.[1] Indeed, it became a confluence of multiple interests.

By the expedition of 1841, referred to earlier, land had been acquired for the establishment of the model farm.[2] Items sold were legitimate goods, which meant that no slaves were sold. It was established by Dr. William Balfour Baikie in 1859 as an anti-slavery outpost and he made it his home. Because Baikie was a naturalist, the city first took such a flavor, thus Sundays were observed as public holidays and it was a resettlement for redeemed slaves. Later, Muslim Hausa traders moved into Lokoja to take advantage of its commercial potentials. But due to the propensity of some of the inhabitants to criminal behavior, Baikie established a consulate to run the affairs in Lokoja and to maintain law and order. A major

---

1. Pedraza, *Story of Lokoja,* 11.
2. See Pedraza, *Story of Lokoja* 20; Ade-Ajayi, *Christian Missions,* 12.

legacy of that consulate is that it established a prison and offenders were punished. M. D. Suleiman notes about this period that "Thieves were flogged publicly in the market and forced to clean the streets of the town. No case of murder was recorded within the period of the consulate."[3] He further draws the contrast that "as soon as the consulate was withdrawn, anarchy reigned within the town and external forces threatened the existence of the young settlement."[4]

This chapter discusses the Christian presence in this place through the Christian Missionary Society (CMS) and the interreligious relationships that began to emerge by 1860. Lokoja Christianity spread around the Niger-Benue Confluence area, and even more significantly became the gateway for the spread of Christianity to Nupe land, Zaria (Wusasa), and the Jos Plateau within the central belt of Nigeria.

In assessing the strategic significance of the Niger-Benue Confluence to the missionary enterprise in Northern Nigeria, Femi Kolapo's comment is noteworthy: "If there was any hope of realizing this dream in the half century before colonization, the CMS stations at Gbebe, Lokoja, and Kippo Hill constituted the clearest, most significant attempts."[5]

Locations that might compare with the distinctive nature of the Lokoja Niger-Benue Confluence area as a missionary, educational, commercial, cultural, and colonial cradle and hub are few. The most obvious in significance is Freetown in Sierra Leone, as a resettlement for liberated slaves, nurtured by Christian institutions such as the famous Fourah Bay College, which became the seedbed of the CMS civilizing mission in West Africa. The Niger-Benue Confluence had a distinctiveness that was sometimes an asset, though at other times it was an impediment to missionary endeavors.

Eugene Stock, the CMS historian, describes the difficult decades of CMS's work in Lokoja. With the Archdeacon Henry

---

3. Suleiman, *Hausa in Lokoja*, 72.

4. Suleiman, *Hausa in Lokoja*, 72.

5. Kolapo, "Christian Missions and Religious Encounters," 513.

Johnson fully assigned to the work in the Upper Niger (as our research area was often generally identified) the historian records:

> At Lokoja, where Johnson ordinarily resided, the work
> was peculiarly difficult, owing to the place being a con-
> fluence, not only of rivers, but still more of languages;
> and this is illustrated by the fact that he had sometimes
> to preach with four interpreters standing by him, trans-
> lating his sentences successively to different sections of
> his congregation. There was also a diversity of religions,
> for here begins the Mohammedan Soudan. In 1883, the
> Society planned a medical mission at Lokoja, and sent
> a young doctor, Percy Brown; but he soon fell sick, was
> put on board ship for England, and died on the voyage.[6]

While the commercial, religious, and colonial factors could
be said to have shaped the entire Lokoja Niger-Benue Confluence communities in different ways, and especially Lokoja town
itself, the missionary activities continued steadily, leaving major
landmarks. Whatever the competing interests and plethora of mo-
tives were imputed into Western presence and the ensuing cultural
conflicts, the missionary legacies are spread all over the area, such
as the iron of liberty which was the point at which slaves were set
free; the Holy Trinity school which was the very first school in
the entirety of Northern Nigeria providing Western education,
and many other primary schools in subsequent decades, located
in such major missionary stations as Kpata, Akabe, Agbaja, Otube,
and Adankolo (a suburb of Lokoja). Even though these schools
were appendages of the churches, they were open to all within the
community who were not necessarily of the Christian faith. By
1964, a mission secondary school—Crowther Memorial College—
had been established which was named after Bishop Crowther, the
great missionary statesman. This shows how revered the name of
Bishop Ajayi Crowther had been, and his indelible influence lives
on in the continued Christian influence in the area. Both Christian and Muslim students have passed through that school and are
making great impact in both the immediate and wider society. The

6. Stock, *Church Missionary Society,* 3:387.

school still stands with the same name, even though the standard has deteriorated steadily since the takeover of mission schools by the government.

The Gains of the Niger Expeditions and the Foundation of Religious Harmony

It may be asked, "What was it that kept the missionary focus unwavering, despite the odds they had to contend with in the area, till the missionary identity of the CMS became an acknowledged fact about the development of the city that is now a state capital?" The missionary activities were sustained through several decades till the Christianity introduced by the CMS (which later metamorphosed into the Anglican Communion) became inseparable from the highpoints of the history of Lokoja and its suburbs in every way.

Following the early expeditions to the Niger, different treaties were established between the rulers along the riverine routes and the British Queen. Around the confluence, the major treaty was with the Ata of Igala Kingdom, who at the time controlled the area. As part of the treaty with the Ata, he was handed a copy of an Arabic Bible containing God's word, which they earnestly hoped he would henceforth follow. The Ata was visibly enthusiastic, and exclaimed, "God bless the Queen." This treaty was considered a significant achievement since the Ata was the most powerful ruler in those parts at the time. This being the main route of slave traffic, the Ata's consent was crucial. The inclusion, in the treaty, of the purchase of a territory for the establishment of the Model Farm from the Ata became like a bonus for this expedition. The location was at the foot of Mount Patti, a well-known and conspicuous mountain in Lokoja, which indeed became the favored location for Lord Lugard's guesthouse. It was also from this location that the British journalist, Flora Shaw, who became Lugard's wife, gave the name Nigeria "Niger Area" in 1914.

It was the next two expeditions—in 1854 and from 1857–1864—that brought the desired triumph both for the explorers and missionaries. The exploring team also desired to establish contact with the Sultan of Sokoto who, according to Pedraza, was "the 'mighty potentate' who held the most important sway in this area of the continent and a satisfactory agreement with him, if achieved, would kill the slave-trade at a blow."[7] Even with this missionary objective, Crowther exercised a great sense of responsibility in relating with other faiths–especially the Muslims whom they called *Mahomettans* or *Mohammedans*. He engaged the services of a Yoruba Muslim by the name Kasumu, who was himself a liberated slave. He was well-versed in Arabic to accompany them on their journeys, especially as one who had appreciated the efforts of the British Government in eradicating slavery, and also the labors of the CMS in converting the heathen to the worship of the one true God. To Crowther's mind, "such a man will do a vast deal in softening the bigotry and prejudice of men of his persuasion."[8] His chosen approach to the religious encounter was clearly stated: "The beginning of our missionary operations under Mohammedan government should not be disputes about the truth or falsehood of one religion or another, but we should aim at toleration, to be permitted to teach their heathen subjects the Religion we profess."[9]

This stated approach by Bishop Crowther from the onset is significant in understanding the long-acknowledged peaceful coexistence of Christianity and the Islamic religion through several generations. It is still common to find most families composed of close relatives from both religions.

One of the most significant accounts is by Bishop Crowther himself. Now consecrated, the bishop delivered his charge to his Synod in 1866. It gives valuable insight about the commencement of missionary work in the confluence during the third exploration of the Niger.

That there was much enthusiasm for this new faith at the point of encounter is apparent from the journals of the native agent, James Ikubaje Thomas, as transcribed by Kolapo. Taking

7. Pedraza, *Story of Lokoja*, 42.
8. Page, *Black Bishop*, 149.
9. Ade-Ajayi, *Christian Missions*, 149.

their base in Gbobe, his journal entries are revealing, like this one in 1858:

> July 13th the Lords day today am very glad to say that our congregation was still improving in this place after service I met with some of them in class three persons were admitted into class again in all 6 in number from Eki people and two Yoruba women. This is our first fruit in this place, also Bassas people came from different villages being market day, they came to see us, so we began to speak to them among whom was Olumody the Chief of Kpata Takum and Kpale the chief of Kpato Kpale they call us loud to come and preach to them[10]

To the north of Lokoja lay the neighboring Oworo land with Agbaja as its principal settlement. The first opportunity of preaching the gospel to them was while *en route* his homeland of Bunu. The journal entry shows that it was received with considerable enthusiasm:

> Dec. 30th Tuesday early in the morning we left Lukoja about 2 o'clock we reached the town by name call Agbaga the place we lodged until in the morning . . . So we stop in the place a little while I went to the chief with my bible I read 3 Chap St. John's gospel 17 to 18 v. all of those hear me they was glad for this good news Jesus Christ set before us in the gospel.[11]

Following the destruction of Gbobe, the mission relocated to Lokoja and paid closer attention to these neighboring settlements. Again, this more definite start of the work at Oworo was welcomed with encouraging comments from James Thomas's journal:

> During the year, before last (1866) our old station Gbebe was destroyed, I came at Lokoja my attention was upon Oworo district until this year they began to enquired what they must do to be saved. Now that part of Oworo

---

10. Kolapo, *Gbebe and Lokoja Journals,* 49.

11. Kolapo, *Gbebe and Lokoja Journals,* 81.

begin to show the little fruit of their beginner 37 persons besides all the attendance.[12]

Special services such as the service of confirmation and even solemnization of holy matrimony were already being celebrated from those early years, showing both acceptance and consolidation of the Christian faith among the indigenes. The journal entry of James Thomas has this:

> The 3rd of Sept 1865 the Lord's day eight persons was confirmed by the bishop of the Niger, the same day 32 persons was admitted sacrament of the Lord's Supper. Many congregation has witnesses for this things. 48, on Monday 4th instant one of our school masters were married in the school room at Gbebe.[13]

Points of Conflict

But it was not all smooth sailing with the other elements in society. We get a picture of the challenges within the context of these early beginnings of Christianity in Lokoja. On 7th November, Saturday, one of their early and ardent converts, a woman named Phoebe Amaya, died after struggling with sickness for about twenty-two days. The testimony about her was that "She was the first party that joined class at Gbebe in 1859 . . . baptized on the 7th Sept 1862 by Bishop Crowther . . . she never was absent from class or Morning Prayer. She very attentive to the means of grace."[14]

An important observation from this account is the real date of the first baptism of converts in Gbobe which had been put at 14th September 1862 in a number of other accounts.[15] It is safe to assume that journal entries from someone of the status of a native evangelist would be subjected to the weaknesses of memory and

12. Kolapo, *Gbebe and Lokoja Journals,* 137.

13. Kolapo, *Gbebe and Lokoja Journals,* 11.

14. Kolapo, *Gbebe and Lokoja Journals,* 141.

15. Crampton, *Christianity in Northern Nigeria,* 19; Page, *Black Bishop,* 180.

are not to be taken in strict exactitude as a major challenge to the other accounts. But following Phoebe's death, the local authorities of King Mashaba claimed that she had owed some money which they insisted must be paid by the CMS agent, James Thomas, on a Sunday. They prevented him from going to church and threatened to exhume her body and to burn it up if he failed to pay the debt there and then. Not even the intervention of the Consul could deter them until some of her few belongings were gathered and handed to the Consul, who sold them to make payment before the creditors relented. That in such a closely knit community as that, no one, whether husband (if not widowed) or relatives, stepped in either to inherit her property or to pay off her indebtedness suggests the estrangement that some of the early converts might have been exposed to.

The next occasion of hostility was on Christmas Day in 1867, when some of the members of the Nupe community who were Muslim attended the service and later their houses were burnt down. We get this from Thomas's journal for the day:

> Rev. J.C. John preached on Friday Dec. 25 being Christmas day. The Service was conducted as usual. The congregation was about 120 persons present, a good many of them being Mahommedans. A great part of them were Nupe of which I interpreted to them. Salamaleku together with some of his men came to church which they never did before; towards the evening greater part of the Nupe's town was burnt down with fire.[16]

No record has been found to reveal the identity of the arsonists who perpetrated this act.

Encounters with the Colonial Administrators

The work in the Lokoja Niger-Benue Confluence had its highs and lows. Eugene Stock, the CMS historian, wrote about the work from the late nineteenth century to the early twentieth century:

16. Kolapo, *Gbebe and Lokoja Journals*, 142.

> . . . good work has been going on in the older parts of
> the Northern Nigeria field, at Lokoja, and in the Nupe
> country, and at Bida, the scenes of many former visits
> by Bishop Crowther in former days. Quite recently, the
> hitherto unpromising outlook has much changed, and a
> widespread spirit of inquiry is now visible, almost like
> that in the Ibo or the Yoruba Country. People are build-
> ing churches and schools for themselves, and begging for
> teachers.[17]

The work in the Lokoja Confluence area came under different administrative arrangements at different times as the missionary structure on ground was modified from time to time. In the
CMS Archives, it is noted that the first place to be occupied in
the Northern Provinces was Lokoja (in 1865), but the mission was
not set apart as an independent unit until April 1907. The main
mission stations were Lokoja (1865), Bassa Country (1897), Bida
(1903), Zaria (1905), and Kano (1921). Work at Panyam, Kabwir,
and Amper, begun by the Cambridge University Missionary Party
in 1907, was handed over to the Sudan United Mission in 1930.

By the last quarter of the nineteenth century, things had
taken a different shape in that the Royal Niger Company under
Goldie had been granted consular powers and they did not want
to be seen to be in association with missionary activities. The period from 1906 to 1912, which preceded the amalgamation of the
Northern and Southern Protectorates by Sir Frederick Lugard, is
one of the most crucial in the history of Nigeria, for it marks both
the beginning of effective administration and the beginning of
the rejection of standards and customs that had endured almost
intact for many centuries. It was the first time that Nigerians were
subjected in any large measure to Western influences, which in
the next fifty years were to have such a great effect on Nigerian
society. A whole new economic world was to be opened to Nigerians. Christianity, as the official doctrine of the colonial masters,
began to spread throughout the 'pagan' areas of both Southern and
Northern Nigeria. New forms of administration and justice were

17. Stock, *Church Missionary Society*, 4:73.

introduced. Finally, education in the Western way of life was made available to a wide range of Nigerians as a result of the spread of missions. So, although this period appears from the annual reports as a static one, it was, in effect, the beginning of silent revolution in Nigeria.[18]

How did the situation in the Niger-Benue Confluence play out with these controversies? General statements and policies had been put in place at various top levels to manage the engagement of missionaries with certain communities, and to bring the different kinds of educational institutions under some colonial administrative supervision. The attention given in this study to education is not to imply that it was the only colonial engagement. Rather it is because CMS strategy placed education as a frontline factor in their engagement with the indigenous society at that time. The CMS strategy was to plant a church and then support it with a school which trained the converts, as well as others in the community who were not among the converts but were interested in Western education for other reasons. Generally, it was seen as a tool to fashion those so educated into suitable assistants for the colonial administration.

In a memo signed by F. D. Lugard, Governor General, dated 8th August 1915, different levels of educational institutions were outlined with the purposes they were meant to achieve. There were:

i. The Technical Institute, which drew boys from provincial schools to spend time in workshops equipped with up-to-date machines driven by electricity and supplied from the source which drives the machinery of the Railway workshops.

ii. The "Gordon College" of Nigeria, which comprised the Secondary School for higher education of native government officials and the Technical Institute, distinct in their aims, yet closely associated in their social life, and "both guided by a common policy in which the formation of character and habits of discipline, honesty and industry are the keynote."

18. Crowder, *Story of Nigeria*, 233.

iii. The Central School of Native Arts and Crafts, intended to foster purely native industries such as native cloth, leather works, basket work, and embroidery, drawing candidates from every province who were interested in such skill acquisition. It was to be financed by the Native Administration, and taught mostly by native craftsmen and probably one British instructor to teach the use of modern tools.

iv. Provincial Schools located at the headquarters of each province. Religious teaching was to be undertaken by "Limams" for Muslim teachers approved by the Emir with the approval of the resident, and in non-Muslim schools the Secretary of State approved the teaching of what they called "undenominational Christianity." For parents who objected to religious instruction, their wards were to be assigned to other tasks during the hour devoted to the teaching of religion.

v. Village Schools. These were to be taught by Native teachers who themselves would have been trained in the government schools.

vi. Mission Schools.[19]

For the purpose of our focus, and given the tone of the comments about it, more of its scope is reproduced here:

> I regard it as an essential feature of a right policy in Education that it should enlist in hearty cooperation all Educational Agencies in the country which are based (as Mission Schools are) on altruistic principles and are conducted with the sole object of benefitting the people . . . As a nation, we have I think failed to appreciate the incalculable importance of guiding and controlling education in the Dependencies and Crown Colonies of the Empire, and are only now realizing and admitting the fact in India, West Africa and elsewhere. Perhaps the results of wrong ideals in education which have produced

19. Lugard, "Mission Schools," 3.

in Germany the terrible experiences of to-day may lead
us at least to appreciate this fact.[20]

With this background, the boundaries appeared defined for
colonial and missionary relationship in their different areas of
operation. But far from being symbiotic, it is on record that the relationship was quite delicate and sometimes even acrimonious, depending on the players in each case. A case in point is the exchange
of correspondence between Miss Matthews, the resident CMS
Missionary in Kpata—one of the early mission stations around the
Niger-Benue Confluence—with one of the colonial officers, the
Divisional Office Touring Officer for her area of ministry.

Naturally the CMS staff saw it as their responsibility to wean
and also protect their converts from pagan ways and from being
victims of the excesses of the native rulers who were exacting more
than was required for poll tax payable to the colonial government.
While the CMS agents were on one side, the colonial government
officials and the native authorities, namely the Gagos (village
heads) and Anaja (village head of Gbobe, the very first mission
settlement on the Confluence) were on the other. Though undesir-
able, this scenario made clear that the impression of positive collaboration by all the whites with the purpose of subjugating the
native population was not entirely accurate.

Contrary to the opinions peddled by critics of foreign missionaries, namely that the missionaries and colonial administrators were collaborators in the exploitation of African resources,
the findings in the Lokoja Niger-Benue Confluence have confirmed that the missionaries and colonial administrators were not
always on the same page. There are numerous instances of the two
parties taking diametrically opposed positions—the missionaries
defending the converts, and the colonialists aligning more with the
traditional authorities.

Apparently, some CMS agents had taken it into their hands
to intercept further payment of what they considered unauthor-
ized tax as this affected church subscription, which also had to be

---

20. Lugard, "Mission Schools," 10.

paid after the government tax. This resulted in the arrest of CMS teachers/evangelists, and the written altercations that followed. Excerpts of these memoranda and correspondence will make the point here. Miss Matthews cites some instances in her letters to the D. O. Touring Officer, Dekina Districts. On 6th November 1931:

i. One of the Hamlet Heads of Emiakpale (a woman) had demanded 3d. per head from her people, over and above their authorized tax, the reason being that Kpata (being £15 short in its tax) had asked her to assist by collecting a further sum of £3, promising that if, another year, Emiakpale was short, Kpata would assist them to make up the money.

ii. The people in Kpata were paying sums over and above their tax—some 9d., some 6d. and some 3d., false tax receipts being given for the sums in question.

iii. The people of Omonoku (Amonoku) were being asked to pay sums over and above their tax, their Hamlet head threatening to have them arrested unless they produced the money at once.

Apparently, she was sure she was helping by reporting these ugly occurrences to the colonial administrators, so she acted swiftly at every fresh episode brought to her notice by the converts. Being white herself, she was seen by most people in the community to be at par with the colonial administrators, having the same powers—only that the Christian converts were her immediate concern, and she needed to prove that she could stand up for them and take up their case with her fellow whites in the colonial administration.

These reports notwithstanding, the colonial administrators found the observations of these CMS missionaries intrusive and irritating, as shown by the tone of their responses at different points. In the first instance, they wanted to uphold the authority of the Anaja and the Gagos, who were the local rulers now being reported, and to whom the missionaries and their converts who felt aggrieved were also being referred. The response of the administrators on the ground was anything but pleasant:

It is most improper that Miss Matthews should interfere in the administration of the District. Unfortunately, she is one of those who are firmly convinced that only a "Christian" can tell the truth whereas in point of fact there is probably nothing to choose between the veracity of the average Catholic, Protestant, Muslim or Pagan, where personal interests are involved . . . There is not the faintest reason why she should mix herself up in any way with either administration or with tax collection. An African "Christian" has, like other humans, two legs and a mouth; and if he has a justifiable complaint (or unjustifiable for the matter of that) there is nothing to prevent his taking his complaint to one of the Touring Officers, to the District Officer or to myself. This is the thirty first year of the Administration of Nigeria by the British Crown and it is absolutely nonsense to maintain that any complainant cannot obtain access to an Administrative Officer . . . Again I learn that an edict has gone forth that whenever a "Christian" is summoned before a Native Tribunal he must be accompanied by a "teacher." The underlying implication that justice is refused to a "Christian" I strongly resent . . . I have caused the District Officer to make it widely known that should such a "teacher" open his mouth and in any way try to interfere with the proceedings he will be summarily dealt with by the Court for contempt.[21]

It was indeed a time of tension between the CMS, the mission agency, and the colonialists, while the natives, divided between the two foreign factions, were caught in the crossfire which destroyed the fabric of their community life and common values.

Some Beneficiaries of the Missionary Training

People traveled from different parts of the Niger-Benue Confluence environment to attend the different institutions set up by the CMS, especially the school for the training of young ladies

21. Smith, "Complaints by and against Christian Converts and Missionaries," 4–5.

who became the wives of the indigenous clergy, and other church workers, or school teachers. Here are a few as they narrated their experiences[22]:

1. Racheal Abenemi, 80 (later got married to an early native educationist, H. T. M. Abenemi): I started infant classes in my village in Oworoland, Igbonla, under Lokoja Local Government today. After I finished infant two I went to Akabe to train under our Mama Miss K. E. Ritsert in January 1941. I was there till first term in the year 1947. That was my experience in school under her before I left to further my education elsewhere. What I can remember was that our Mama had a steady program for every day. For school days and Saturdays everybody knew what he was going to do for each day. On Saturday we used to have a choir practice and on Sunday evenings we went to church, and we used to learn some memory verses every Sunday. Anybody who failed to memorize or recite her own after service will be delayed from taking her lunch until you are able to recite them. On Sunday evenings we gathered at Mama's parlor where we would sing choruses and she taught us so many songs.

2. Rebecca Kato, 81, who became the wife of the B. A. Kato who rose to the position of an Archdeacon in some locations around the Niger-Benue Confluence, said, "Miss Ritsert was a missionary, she sent us to school and took care of children as a missionary."

3. Mrs. Monica Yacim, 78: During my time with the missionary Miss Ritsert, we were about eighty girls (80) with her. While some were leaving upon their graduation, some were coming in. I came to Akabe in 1935 and I left Akabe in 1946. I did up to class five (5) being that there was no class six then, and girls education was not important to some of our people

22. Interviews 1–5 come from a group interview which was conducted on May 19, 2009, while the sixth interview was performed separately on May 27, 2014.

then, so I left to marry in 1946. (She got married to Mr. J. A. Yacim, who became a seasoned civil servant.)

4. Mrs. Dora Abraham, approximately 80: When we were at Akabe we were taught so many things including domestic work, vocational works like knitting and other hand works. On Saturdays after our devotion and breakfast, our Mama used to divide us into four groups, one group will collect all our clothes together for washing in the stream, and the second group would go to fetch firewood. On Sundays we went to church for Sunday worship, and then learnt some memory verses. After we returned from the church service, we had to recite the memory verses, and if you cannot, then your lunch will be suspended until you are able to recite it before you take your lunch.

5. Angelina Yacim, 74: I was born in 1935, and my mother died two months after my birth, so I was taken to Akabe to Miss Ritsert who took care of me from that infancy. During my time we were like six orphans who she was raising, and she looked after us. I grew to meet her teaching people how to conduct orderly worship. People like Pa Kato (who later rose to the position of an Archdeacon) were with her and she also taught them how to sing in parts.

6. Comfort Ndagi, 79, attended the same school from 1943–44. She traveled from Nupe land to Akabe in the Niger-Benue Confluence mission area with some other girls. Because the boarding school for the boys was in Bida, the girls were sent to Akabe. Altogether it took three days journey, starting by lorry from Bida to Badegi. They then took the train from there to Baro, then continued from Baro to Lokoja by boat which they called ships. (These vessels were named variously after Clapperton, Lander, and some of the early explorers). From Lokoja, they traveled by paddle canoe to Shintaku, and then trekked to Akabe. Altogether it took about 3 day's journey. She also described her experience of the school: "Miss Ritsert was making our dresses. Early in the morning

we would wake up, take our buckets and containers to fetch water. This was about 5.00-6.00 am. Then we would take our bath while those cooking would be busy with the water we had brought. School started at 8.00 am. We did not pray in our rooms, but at the assembly where we lined up according to sizes, and marched into class. We had bout 4–5 classes. We had no reading book. Nupe Bible was the reading book. Nupe was the medium of expression. Other activities were Singing, Arithmetic, Christian Religious Studies, while older ones were taught a stitching style called 'smoking' (an intricate pattern by needlework). When we wore our attire, we looked like angels in those attires. Each class had about 20–25 pupils. One of the teachers was Mr. Obada. We spent two years"

It is noteworthy that she became the wife of Jonathan Ndagi, former Nigerian Ambassador to Australia, and pioneer Vice Chancellor of the Federal University of Technology in Minna. His father, Rev. Paul Birama Ndagi, had been a Muslim convert who himself persecuted Christians. After his conversion, his three wives deserted him. On account of the persecution he also suffered, Mr. Alvarez advised him to go to Lokoja in February 1923. There he met a young lady, Comfort, who agreed to marry him. From this marriage, Jonathan Ndagi was born in October 1928. He returned to Nupe land where he evangelized for many years, using Katcha as his base. He was ordained as a priest on October 18, 1955 at St. Paul's Church, Jos. He was aged seventy-two. He says of that milestone in his life, "I count this as one of the greatest events and privileges (sic) of my life. Though old I hope by the grace of God to play my part in the Master's vineyard"[23]

The Arrival of Other Mission Churches

The CMS was for a long time the only mission church in Lokoja. From the time of their establishment as a mission station in 1858, and the Holy Trinity Church (now Cathedral) in 1865, the next

23. Crampton, *Christianity in Northern Nigeria*, 120.

denomination to be established was the Roman Catholic Mission in 1884. Their main activities were planting churches, providing Western education and health centers, and modeling better agricultural practices. Even though Islam and traditional religion were on the ground, the missionaries were cautious, diplomatic, and respectable in their dealings. From the earliest stages when Samuel Ajayi Crowther was the arrowhead, respect for other religious persuasions was a cardinal principle. Commenting on this disposition of Crowther and his workers, Ayandele points out that "patience, amiableness, sympathy, and forbearance were their watchwords."[24] He was so trusted and in powerful control that the entire area came to have great confidence in Crowther. Indeed Ayandele further notes that he became, "perhaps the most powerful external influence on the Muslim rulers of the Nupe country between 1869 and 1888" and that, in fact, "the Emir allowed him to draw up the constitution by which Jacob Meheux Musa, a liberated Muslim African, administered Lokoja until the days of Goldie's Royal Niger Company."[25] This, in addition to the fact that the princes of the ruling house in Lokoja were educated by the CMS most likely accounts for the legendary harmonious relationship between the successive traditional rulers of Lokoja and the Anglican Church and Christian community generally. Indeed, a sizable number of Anglicans are among the key traditional title holders.

The Roman Catholic Mission

As noted above, the Roman Catholic Mission was the next mission church to come to Lokoja. They started by organizing Vicarates and Prefectures. The first of these was the Prefecture Apostolic of the Niger, with its headquarters in Lokoja, created in 1884.[26] There was excitement about their arrival in Lokoja, where they were warmly received by M. Matteri, agent-in-chief of the French company who

24. Ayandele, "Missionary Factor," 136.
25. Ayandele, "Missionary Factor," 505.
26. Crampton, *Christianity in Northern Nigeria*, 154.

provided accommodation. Soon however, malaria—that dreaded disease—descended on them, as noted by Father Poirier in his journal of November 25, 1884:

> The fever has come upon us. I have had three attacks. Father Fiorentini has one at the moment. Father Piolat had been very ill but has recovered. Commandant Matteri has saved us from great misery. Lokoja is not very important, but it is a strategical point for trade and missions, so that we must establish ourselves here.[27]

Along the same lines, Fr. James Higgins, SMA, corroborates the account above:

> It was in 1882 that Monsignor Jean-Baptiste Chausse SMA, the Prefect-Apostolic of the Catholic Church in Lagos, and Father Theodore Holley SMA, of Abeokuta fame, sailed up the River Niger to assess the possibility of bringing knowledge of Christ to the people who lived east and north of Yoruba land . . . covering all that territory in modern Nigeria, north of Lokoja, an important trading center at the confluence of the two biggest rivers in West Africa, the Niger and the Benue. The Evangelization of that vast territory was assigned to the Society of African Missions (SMA). In November 1884 SMA Fathers Jules Poirier, Filippo Fiorentini and Pierre Piolat arrived by boat in Lokoja, where they set up their temporary headquarters from which they hoped to evangelize the towns and villages north of the two rivers.[28]

They too had their early share of casualties, for Father Fiorentini died there in October 1884, and was replaced by Father Andrew Dorman of Belfast the following month.

The relationship with the CMS which they met on the ground was cordial, and has remained so. In his *History of the Cathedral Church of the Holy Trinity, Lokoja*, Micah Amihere notes that "when the Roman Catholic Mission came from Onitsha to Lokoja in 1884, it was, for eleven years, accommodated on Holy Trinity

27. Bane, *Catholic Pioneers*, 165.

28. Higgins, "History of the Church," 1.

Church compound, that is, from 1884–1895."[29] In 1888, the head-quarters of the Prefecture Apostolic of the Niger was moved outside the North to Asaba from where it was henceforth administered.

The Baptist Church

After nearly three decades, the Baptist Church came into Lokoja in 1913 through some Yoruba traders from Ogbomosho. Indeed, this was the pattern of spread into the North, particularly after the amalgamation of the Northern and Southern protectorates in 1914. These traders were the lay evangelists, and Lokoja was seen as a stranger-friendly settlement which was also peaceful for business-inclined people. Like the Roman Catholic Mission before them, they also started by worshipping with the Holy Trinity Church. However, they nursed a desire—which was soon fulfilled—for their distinctive Baptist method of liturgical and worship expression. There were seven people who became recognized as the founding fathers of the first Baptist church in Lokoja: Ezekiel Oyekan, Solomon Oyedokun, Samuel Agboola, Emmanuel Leke, Daniel Olaleye, Joseph Olaniyan, and Josiah Bolaji.[30]

The Aladura Revival

Besides the mission churches, the *Aladura* revival in Yorubaland of the 1930s also spread its influence to the Niger-Benue Confluence. J. D. Y. Peel notes that "The revival attracted huge numbers of people from as far away as Ilorin, Ijebu or even across the Niger, and caused serious disruption of transport and food supplies, which brought it to the notice of the authorities."[31] Furthermore, Peel records that Joseph Babalola, the founder of Aladura, went around Ilesha several times in the day, clad in white shorts and shirt, with Bible and hand bell, "preaching to the people to renounce

---

29. Amihere, *History of the Cathedral Church*, 4.

30. Ajala and Ajagbe, *First Baptist Church*, 7.

31. Peel, *Aladura*, 91.

evil practices and witchcraft, and to bring out for burning all their idols and *juju*, for God was powerful enough to answer all their needs."[32] This Aladura revival spread like wildfire, and Crampton records that Igbirraland was visited by an Aladura missionary in 1930, and that "objects of pagan worship were cast away as 'bad medicine.'"[33] A great number of Christian believers in Lokoja at this time who were mostly Anglicans went to these miracle movements without being hindered by the CMS missionaries. However, the colonial administrators were skeptical and even implied that such visits to those they regarded as charlatans were major distractions from their civic responsibilities. For instance, the colonial administrators—notably E. V. Rochfort Rae, Acting Resident for Kabba Province, and G. Miles Clifford, District Officer in charge of Igala Division—made references to the Ikare revival in some of their correspondence. Their opinion became apparent when Bishop Alfred Smith, who had charge of the CMS missionaries in this area, wrote to protest the arrest of some CMS evangelists by the hostile colonial administrators. The response of Mr. Rae, dated 10th December 1931, reveals his disgust:

> I have to inform you that the root of the trouble is the disastrous pilgrimage of the people of Bassa Nge to the charlatan at Ikare earlier in the year. This movement which was most unfortunately fostered and encouraged by CMS Teachers and Pastors has resulted in the pauperisation of those who were foolish enough to listen to their advice. The collection of the tax for 1931/32 which would otherwise have been of no hardship—incidentally it is just about the same amount as your mission demands per annum from its adherents—has therefore become extremely difficult.[34]

Modern-day Lokoja still witnesses early morning *Aladura* devotees, with hand bell, occasionally going round major streets, calling people to repentance.

---

32. Crampton, *Christianity in Northern Nigeria*, 142.

33. Peel, *Aladura*, 142.

34. Provincial Correspondence, NAK, Jacket 95/1928.

These early beginnings were devoted to strict Anglican practice of the Christian faith. Nevertheless, the arrival of the younger missionaries who were described by Ade-Ajayi as "able, young, zealous, impetuous, uncharitable and opinionated,"[35] and better known in the historical records of this period as the Cambridge seven turned the tide, for they were more interested in evangelical spirituality than church order. This was indicative of the ecclesiastical disposition of most of the missionaries in the service of the CMS. Initially, Northern Nigeria was under Bishop Crowther's vast and unwieldy Diocese of Western Equatorial Africa beyond the Queen's Dominions, but with the Niger Mission crisis that led up to his death in 1891, and with the Niger Delta Pastorate becoming an independent administration, the diocese became known as Diocese of Western Equatorial Africa. The Rt. Rev. J. S. Hill, DD, was the bishop from 1893–1894, followed by the long episcopate of the Rt. Rev. Herbert Tugwell, DD, from 1894–1919. The significant development in the Anglican Church at this time is captured by Ade-Ajayi: "The Bishopric of Lagos was at last created in 1894 to oversee the Yoruba Mission, the Niger Mission and Lower Niger, and the Niger territories of Northern Nigeria."[36] All this while, from the start of missionary work in Nigeria and consolidation efforts, the Anglican Church was administered from Sierra Leone. This covered the period from 1852–1979. In 1919, Melville Jones was made Bishop of Lagos, covering all but the eastern part of Nigeria. In 1925, Alfred Smith was consecrated as Assistant Bishop of Lagos, charged with special responsibility for Northern Nigeria, where the Niger-Benue Confluence area belonged. Since the posture of the colonial administrators was unfavorable for additional missionary personnel to Dr. Miller, who had a special concession, Bishop Smith chose Ilorin as his base. According to Crampton, "the work in the North was divided into four with four superintendents: Alvarez for Lokoja, Wedgewood for Plateau, Thomson for Nupe and Miller for the Hausa District."[37] Eventually more

35. Ade-Ajayi, *Christian Missions*, 250.

36. Omoyajowo, *Anglican Church in Nigeria*, xiiiix.

37. Crampton, *Christianity in Northern Nigeria*, 132.

Dioceses were inaugurated in Nigeria between 1951 and 1977, including the Diocese of Northern Nigeria which was inaugurated on 30th January 1954, with Bishop J. E. L. Mort as the first Diocesan Bishop. On 24th February 1979, the Anglican Church in Nigeria became an autonomous province.

From the foregoing, it is evident that the faith as taught by the CMS had been embraced in the locality with credible and sustained visible impacts. A major hindrance was the militancy of the jihadist expeditions of the Etsu Massaba of Nupe, even though it was apparent that his greater motive was commercial rather than religious. There were also the difficult days of the Niger Mission crisis culminating in the death of Ajayi Crowther in 1891, and the apparent hostility of the colonial administrators. Indeed, by the beginning of the twentieth century, Thomas Walter Bako, identified by Elizabeth Isichei as "an Oworro Yoruba who had been enslaved as a child and redeemed by a missionary at Lokoja"[38] became an evangelist. He was killed while returning from an evangelistic outreach to Tawari village, near Koton Karfe in 1903, thus becoming the first known Christian martyr in Northern Nigeria, next to Joshua Hart of Bonny in the Niger Delta. This shows how rooted Christianity was in the heart of early converts in Lokoja, albeit most would have been ex-slaves.

There is therefore no doubt that Lokoja and its hinterlands were not only the first Christianized areas of Northern Nigeria, but significantly their Christian influence stretched beyond the central belt of Nigeria. Most missionary societies that began work in Northern Nigeria started off in Lokoja. These include the Sudan Interior Mission (SIM), the Sudan United Mission (SUM), the United Missionary Society (UMS), and the Cambridge Universities Missionary Party (CUMP). It is no wonder that Lokoja became the first preferred ecumenical center in Northern Nigeria for the meeting of the Protestant missions in Northern Nigeria in July 1910. This maiden meeting was attended by representatives from the CMS, and other missions like SUM, SIM, and CMM (the Canadian Mennonite Mission). They discussed and resolved

38. Isichei, *Varieties of Christian Experience in Nigeria*, 71.

matters of common concern touching on the social and spiritual life of African converts, missionary reactions to unfavorable British colonial policies, and the establishment of the Niger Press for the printing of Christian Literature. Other aspects covered were matters of church organization, training of native helpers, polygamy, wives for the converts, the dowry, the posture one should take in prayer, a common outline for worship, Scripture translation, language study, grants-in-aid for schools, and liquor traffic. Among the resolutions were that vernacular was favored as the medium of instruction in mission schools, and African Christians were to be dissuaded from using English attire.[39] All these attest to the importance that the early missionary activities had bestowed on Lokoja, which must have accounted for the colonial presence and subsequent location of Lord Lugard's important political landmarks such as the amalgamation of the Northern and Southern Protectorates in 1914, making Lokoja not only a state capital, a diocesan headquarters, and the headquarters of the Ecclesiastical Province of Lokoja, but indeed the first political capital of Nigeria.

39. Grimley and Robinson, *Church Growth in Central and Southern Nigeria*, 77–78; Turaki, *Theory and Practice of Christian Missions in Africa*, 435–36; Hewitt, *Problems of Success*, 73.

Chapter 3

COLONIAL POLICIES *and* MISSIONARY EDUCATION

(1872–1940)[1]

IT SHOULD BE NOTED FROM the outset that the mission agencies saw as their primary goal the evangelization of the indigenous population in their places of assignment. The educational component was seen only as a necessary subsidiary to facilitate literacy, especially in Bible reading for the purpose of spiritual nurture for the converts. The recruitment of educational experts was therefore not considered as much a priority in mission work as those trained in theology and medicine. What was introduced to the mission fields by way of education came as a response to felt needs.

It is almost impossible to discuss the missionary encounter in the Lokoja Niger-Benue Confluence area, as indeed all of Africa, without paying particular attention to the education sector. Its role has become pivotal and has been interpreted in different ways by different interest groups. In this regard the following critical comment by Lamin Sanneh is pertinent:

> No single subject has attracted as much consistent attention and resources in the history of Christian penetration

1. First published as "Assessing Colonial Involvement," 1–19.

of Africa as education, and no subject was as effective in the revolutionary transformation of African societies. Consequently, education assumed a wide range of roles. In the hands of the missionaries, it was often used as an instrument of conversion and nurture . . . In the hands of conservative and some liberal philanthropists, education was conceived as a means of social control, to instil in the African a proper attitude of subservience towards the white man . . . Then again, in the eyes of the traditional Muslim leaders, modern education represented the scourge of infidel Christians, and it was approached with the greatest defiance or reluctance. Finally, for many African populations . . . education was welcomed as the gateway to a new and secure future. In all these instances modern education produced results and repercussions far greater than could be envisaged from any single standpoint.[2]

When the colonial government considered it necessary to become involved in education, they also became the regulatory body for all educational initiatives by setting the standards, providing grants-in-aid, and ensuring appropriate supervision. It became mandatory, therefore, for the mission agencies to raise their educational standards to match the expectations of the colonial government. For the CMS work in West Africa—notably the Niger Mission—as also in East Africa, it was a time of returning to the drawing board to rethink their objectives in mission and what adjustments were considered necessary. As they found out, there were no ready-made answers. The most challenging aspect was in ascertaining what kind of candidates they should recruit for the missionary education sector. The combination of evangelistic zeal and educational professionalism was not readily present in every missionary or even most of those available for recruitment. To resolve this singular challenge, conferences were held to determine what adjustments and possible compromises in missionary policies were considered necessary in this process.

2. Sanneh, *West African Christianity*, 127.

The Early Missionary Education Scenario

From the early stages, the role and extent of missionary education needed to be clearly defined. Ayandele observes that the founders of Western education were divided into two schools of thought, namely, the liberal and conservative groups: "The more liberal group favored fully-fledged school curricula, but the more conservative and dogmatic group doubted whether the Western education being introduced into Africa should ever be encouraged to go beyond the three R's and a narrowly conceived Bible-tied curriculum."[3]

The conservative group had restricted views about the purpose of man's existence on earth. This perspective Ayandele termed "narrow-minded and bigoted."[4] In their view, all that mattered was that man should be so heavenly minded as contained in the Bible, which was the "Book of Books,"[5] and the one literature that the convert should read as the guiding principle of all his actions. To make him read literature on, or acquire knowledge of, "this sinful world"[6] or the universe would amount to diverting his soul away from focusing on the heavenly vision.

From the onset of missionary education in Nigeria in the 1840s, the curriculum, according to Ade-Ajayi, was centered on the four Rs (Ayandele has "three R's") namely: Religion, Reading, Writing and Arithmetic (also referred to as Ciphering). A typical day in a mission school included singing, Rehearsals of Scripture passages, grammar, reading, spelling, writing, and geography in the morning hours until noon. In the afternoons till they closed at about 4:00pm they added arithmetic to more reading and spelling lessons.[7]

For a number of reasons, in particular the presence of Quranic schools in the communities, Western education was late

3. Ayandele, *African Historical Studies*, 80.
4. Ayandele, *African Historical Studies*, 80.
5. Ayandele, *African Historical Studies*, 80.
6. Ayandele, *African Historical Studies*, 80.
7. Ade-Ajayi, *Christian Missions*, 138.

in developing in Northern Nigeria. According to Crampton, the Quranic schools numbered about 25,000 at this time.[8] Another factor was the general aversion of the colonial officers to missionary presence in the "Muslim North,"[9] which had the concomitant effect of restricting Western missionary education in Northern Nigeria, even though it had been beneficial in the South.

As already noted, education for missionary discipleship purposes had been a cardinal component of the missionary enterprise from the earliest times. Both the Protestant and Roman Catholic mission agencies had become quite convinced about the place of education at different levels as the gateway to civilization among the converts who needed to read the Bible and be literate in other ways. Indeed, as early as 1857, Bowen, a pioneer Baptist missionary, had noted,

> Our designs and hopes in regard to Africa are not simply to bring as many individuals as possible to the knowledge of Christ. We desire to establish the Gospel in the hearts and minds and social life of the people, so that truth and righteousness may remain and flourish among them, without the instrumentality of foreign missionaries. This cannot be done without civilization. To establish the Gospel among any people, they must have Bibles and therefore must have the art to make them or the money to buy them. They must read the Bible and this implies instruction.[10]

This defined the focus of missionary education to be limited to the introduction of literacy, the training of agents and the provision of such education as would empower the people to read Bibles or purchase them. Early literacy was focused on the study of Nigerian languages, thereby pioneering the development of indigenous grammar and the written form (orthography) with varying degrees of success. Of course, there was not always a ready acceptance of this education by the communities, especially because the

8. Crampton, *Christianity in Northern Nigeria,* 98.

9. Crampton (2004), *Christianity in Northern Nigeria,* 98.

10. Bowen, *Adventures and Missionary Labours,* 323.

young people were the labor force on the farms, and some chiefs, especially in the Delta areas, even expected to be paid for releasing their wards to the missionaries. On the other hand, the missionaries themselves considered their primary aim to be the teaching of the adult converts to be able to read the Bible in their native languages, so that they would in turn instruct their own children and dependents.

According to Townsend, "To the same extent that the adult population are brought under Christian instruction will children and other dependents be brought under instruction likewise."[11] This gave rise to the Sunday school, where the adult converts who were not available for the daily school in the week could be taught. This also placed missionary emphasis on the translation of the Bible into the vernacular, as they limited their efforts to the simplicity of orthography that did not task the adult mind too much. In some of the early CMS mission stations, like Abeokuta, evening adult literacy classes were added during the week. In this way, the early converts were able to read in the vernacular and become familiar with some parts of the Bible, such as the Gospel of Mark, or the Catechism, which set out the basic doctrines of the Christian faith. They also learnt some popular hymns. Their emphasis on the preservation of the vernacular—sometimes even against the wishes of their converts and the unenthusiastic posture of the colonial administrators who were more inclined to the use of the English language—remains the unparalleled merit of the missionaries. Indeed, Ayandele attributes the evolution of modern Nigeria to the efforts of the missionaries: "It was upon them almost entirely that the social and moral development of the Nigerian peoples fell in the period ending in 1914."[12]

Where there was a desire for education of children, as in the city states of the Niger Delta, the interest of the adult in sending them to the mission schools was not so much to learn Christianity, but rather to supplement the system of socialization and apprenticeship already built into them. This was a system of acquiring

11. CMS CA2/085.

12. Ayandele, *Missionary Impact*, 283.

necessary skills within the community. They therefore saw missionary education as providing the additional skills of reading and writing which they desired for their own local needs such as gauging palm-oil, building boats, or manufacturing gun powder. That notwithstanding, the missionaries were hopeful, seeing in the schools the seedbed of the emerging church. To all the mission agencies, the primary objective of providing Western education was religious instruction, especially targeting the young children who were to be weaned from the pagan ideas of their parents. Through the schools and the churches, the missionaries sought to effect moral and social transformation. A common inducement to ensure steady commitment of the pupils in those days was for the missionaries to train them and have them reside in the mission compounds. This gave rise to boarding schools, which soon became popular, though quite expensive to run.

The Phases of Missionary Education in Lokoja

Missionary education in the Lokoja Niger-Benue Confluence stations can be classified into three major phases. The first stage (1857–1864) covers the period of activities in the first mission station at Gbobe, which was started in 1858 and where eventually the first baptism in Northern Nigeria was conducted on 14th September 1862.[13] It was also at that same location that Bishop Crowther confirmed a group of Sierra Leonean settlers and native converts in 1864, quite likely the first confirmation service in Northern Nigeria, and probably among the first after his own consecration as bishop that same year (29th June 1864). The education provided there at this stage was mainly elementary education geared toward the reading of the Bible by the converts. Those who were at the helm of this initiative were the native agents, notably James Thomas Ikubaje, Edward Cline, and Thomas Joseph. According to

13. McKenzie *Inter-religious Encounters*, 41.

Kolapo, they started the first Western-style institutional education in central Nigeria.[14]

The second stage covers the period from the establishment of the Holy Trinity School in Lokoja by Bishop Crowther in 1865 to the time when the *Preparandi,* ably built by Archdeacon Johnson as a vocational training institution patterned after the initiatives in Fourah Bay, was sold by the overzealous missionaries of the Sudan Party in 1890.[15]

The third stage falls within the period of metamorphosis in mission educational policies, resulting in a transition from sole missionary control to a partnership with the colonial government within the context of the Niger Mission, and the CMS Northern Nigeria from about 1908–1940.

A Paradigm Shift

The colonial government did not get involved in education until 1872, when it began to provide a grant of £30 to each of the three missionary agencies operating within the colony of Lagos: the CMS, the Wesleyan Methodist Church, and the Southern Baptist Convention. Hitherto, these mission agencies had established, financed, and managed primary school education with the assistance of the local community and converts. Two years later, by 1874, government subvention rose to £100 per mission. This continued until 1882, when the colonial government enacted the Education Ordinance that was binding on all the British colonies of Lagos, Ghana, The Gambia, and Sierra Leone. This became a regulatory act which affected all the missionary agencies in the Southern Protectorate of Nigeria. According to Uruakpa, "To establish any schools from then, certain conditions were to be met. Qualification for Grants was based again on certain criteria,

---

14. Kolapo, "CMS and the Failure of Christian Transition," 17.

15. Crampton, *Christianity in Northern Nigeria,* 26.

especially payment and the quality of the school's examination results."[16]

As the colonies became more politically assertive, even though independence was still a long way off, the need to put in place structures to ensure the emergence of a crop of native leadership became even more pressing. Appropriate attention has been devoted to the missionary factor in the making of a new elite and in its sociopolitical impact, notably by Ajayi, Ayandele, Isichei, Tasie, and a few others. But as the lines between colonial and missionary concerns became more pronounced, the two bodies had to forge some meeting points to harmonize their divergent objectives.

More than is often acknowledged, education by missionaries came to occupy a major place that could almost be described as center stage in the 1930s. This transition of interest and focus was precipitated by the government's new policies regarding partnership with missionaries in the area of education. With all that had been done, the CMS observed in June 1937 that, in the task known as the "refashioning of African life,"[17] there was the need for them to properly articulate the role of missionary education. Almost all mission agencies working in Africa at that time were addressing the same concerns about the place of education in the missionary praxis. This necessitated several joint meetings by mission agencies working in Africa. A supervisor of schools became indispensable to the whole mission structure. Interpreting this in the Niger Mission context, the Rev. E. F. Wilkinson wrote that its aim was "To make education in mission schools fully efficient, i.e., that they are effective in building up fine, Christian character, alive to the needs of their land and trained to take their full share in their country's progress."[18] The Rev. J. M. Carr followed up these thoughts in the same setting a few months later with this observation:

> Education in Nigeria is still in its infancy, in the stage of experiment in the building up of organization and technique. In many parts it is still in the pioneer stage

16. Uruakpa, "Anglican Church and Educational Development," 135.

17. Church Missionary Society, "Missionary Supervisor of Schools," 1.

18. Wilkinson, "Missionary Supervisor of Schools," 1.

of small beginnings, the building of village schools and the finding and training of teachers to staff them. To be a pioneer of schools means to be a pioneer in African Education. It is a Missionary job of first importance, for the Christian schools of to-day are building the Christian Church of to-morrow, and will determine the quality of the Africa which is to be.[19]

It had certainly become a settled matter that education was an integral part of missionary work.

While the earliest secondary grammar school established by the CMS on 25 March 1845 in Sierra Leone attracted students from all over Africa, and West Africa in particular, other initiatives in Nigeria followed from the 1850s onwards, continuing to Abeokuta, Lagos, Onitsha, Bonny, Warri, Sapele, and Ijebu right into the early part of the twentieth century.

The Holy Trinity CMS school was established in 1865 in Lokoja as an elementary school. The situation and ethos of missionary education as described above was not different in the mission stations around Lokoja. Missionary education in the Lokoja Niger-Benue confluence area is among the earliest in the Niger Mission, dating to the second half of the nineteenth century. However, the growth rate of the Holy Trinity School did not reflect much enthusiasm on the part of the residents. From the eleven pioneer pupils of 1865, there were just about thirty to forty pupils on the roll by 1871, supported only by skeletal educational activities in the satellite mission stations of Gbobe and Kippo Hill.[20]

By 1900, the CMS presence on the confluence had clocked over four and a half decades since the first mission station at Gbobe in 1858. It had been nine years since Bishop Crowther's death in the heat of the crisis in the Niger Mission. This unhappy atmosphere did not exclude Lokoja, which was then known as the Upper Niger.

19. Church Missionary Society, "Missionary Supervisor of Schools," 1.
20. Crampton, *Christianity in Northern Nigeria*, 21–22.

The Period of Crisis in Missionary Education

By July 1926, the CMS came to terms with the fact that their ministry had to undergo a major review of strategy if they were to remain relevant. The method hitherto had been to have what they called single-man stations in which wide areas of population were targeted for missionary influence. The general response to the missionary encounter had been enthusiastic until the Niger mission crisis and the humiliation of Bishop Crowther sparked outrage from many quarters, with its many consequences of breakaways and Ethiopianism. The nurture of native believers to maturity—otherwise referred to as discipleship in mission circles—was clearly not commensurate with the crowd of adherents, for the size of converts outdistanced the best efforts of the few European missionaries on the ground in most mission stations. This was compounded since native hands had been largely discredited in the crisis surrounding the ministry of Bishop Crowther, especially with the well-known scandals surrounding a number of his staff, which became strong ammunition for his critics. The missionaries further observed that these "unwieldy congregations afforded a growing menace to the welfare and purity of corporate Christian life and evoked expressions of increasing concern from European missionaries"[21] whose hands were too full to properly attend to this.

For the CMS, this new problem surfaced in different ways. In East Africa, for instance, more intensive training of native leaders had to await government subsidy of missionary education in the form of grants-in-aid. While this was primarily intended to foster secular education, it provided leeway for the essential character-building content to be contributed by missionary influence. This factor explained missionary enthusiasm.

For well over a decade hence, this situation made the missionary agencies sit up to match the expectations of the government. Uruakpa further notes that:

---

21. Hooper, "Present Crisis," 1.

In almost all her schools the Anglican Mission made serious efforts to raise the quality of her schools and staff strength through Teacher-Training Programmes including a number of other managerial skills that could commend her performance in education.[22]

While the missionaries sought a way to make the most of this situation, the government of the colonies had to ensure that their subsidies were applied strictly toward raising educational standards, especially in the development of boarding schools, which appeared to be the ideal. But it was expensive as a missionary project. To accommodate the implications of these adjustments in mission policy, the missionaries had to put in place some administrative safeguards as indicated below to ensure prudent application of their limited resources and to avoid what Hooper called "too extensive domination" or even the hijacking of their primary motive of training by government.[23]

The CMS was hard-pressed to meet up with the expectations implicit in the acceptance of government assistance. Their staff and the newly recruited missionaries lacked the technical competence or spiritual qualification required for the systematic training of native leadership. In view of this crisis, the CMS felt a need to seriously modify their policy to enable them to fill up the positions being opened to them by the government. They were particularly concerned that their response should not necessitate a reversal of government policy and the introduction of an educational system independent of missionary input. Should that ever happen, they feared that the consequences would be incalculable: "we shall witness the ghastly tragedy of secular education offered to people whose instinctive thought and practice introduce religious conceptions into every activity of life."[24] Further, they would forfeit the opportunity of influencing even secular education to produce Christian leadership in all aspects of human endeavor. That was not all, for they stood the risk of also forfeiting the confidence of

22. Uruakpa, "Anglican Church and Educational Development," 135.

23. Hooper, "Present Crisis," 3.

24. Hooper, "Present Crisis," 4.

the converts who had owed much of their upbringing to the missionaries. And since other mission agencies appeared to be matching government expectation, it was imperative on the CMS to do all it could to justify the high trust placed in them. They therefore considered the option of asking the field executives to assign European missionaries to supervisory roles in order to allow native leadership to emerge as proposed much earlier by Henry Venn in his three-selfs policy.

To consolidate these arrangements, a scheme for supervision of mission schools by missionaries in cooperation with the government was launched. By this arrangement, the salaries and all related expenses of the missionaries were to be borne by government. The CMS Parent Committee seconded Rev. E. J. Evans, then with the Yoruba Mission, and Mr. E. F. Wilkinson of the Niger Mission, from their primary mission duties to take on these roles, while their mission responsibilities were to be advertised for new recruits to take up. This was by no means limited to the mission stations in West Africa. Indeed, it was a season of change in missionary focus and strategy in almost all areas of CMS engagement. In a conference held at the Church Missionary House, 6 Salisbury Square on 16th June 1926, the focus was exclusively on Christian education in East Africa. At that conference, Mr. Oldham sought to invite an optimistic outlook by persuading the conference that the invitation to partnership by the government had the potential to influence the new civilization that was rapidly taking place in Africa with Christian values which would raise a crop of African Christian leaders for both the church and civil society.

Missionary Education in the CMS Niger Diocese

The Lokoja Niger-Benue Confluence area is located within the Upper Niger Diocese of the missionary enterprise of CMS. The Niger Diocese itself covered these government provinces: Onitsha, part of Owerri, part of Benin, and part of Warri, with each of these provinces further divided into districts which were virtually the same as the mission districts. The CMS resolved to avoid duplication of efforts where there were schools already established by either the government or the Roman Catholic Church. The schools which they established for each of these groups were mainly in four categories, the highest level being the Central School, also called Standard VI:

i. The *Religious Schools* which were conducted by native agents such as catechists and evangelists in the villages. The medium of teaching was the vernacular. The subjects were: Bible reading, writing, counting, singing and basic hygiene, and teaching lasted for two hours daily.

ii. The *Sub-standard Vernacular Schools* were slightly a step further than the religious schools and were mainly a local initiative intended for those children who did not intend to leave their villages.

iii. The 3rd and 2nd *Grade Schools* were designed as intermediate level schools going up to Standards II, III, or IV. Those who taught in the 2nd grade schools must have passed Standard VI, while those appointed as headmasters at this level must have passed the 1st- and 2nd-year pupil teacher examinations, though a majority had not received any specialized training in an institution.

iv. The 1st *Grade or Central School* was more expensive to maintain. The headmasters at this level were trained, certified teachers assisted by two or more trained hands, depending on the size of the schools. More careful attention seemed to have been given to this level, as the mission resolved that it aimed at "giving every boy who is desirous and capable of reaching Standard VI an opportunity of doing so in a natural way, without the difficulties of largely increased fees or absence from home."[25]

Indeed, plans were afoot to keep pace with the high demand for missionary education by increasing the number of Assisted

25. Church Mission House Memo, "Missionary Education in the Niger Diocese," 2.

Standard VI schools to thirty within five years (i.e., by 1935), with a minimum of four certified teachers to each school. In the same vein, the addition of Standard VII was being contemplated for some schools, in order to provide an appropriate level of education to gain government employment in some areas. An added reason was to stop what they called "the great rush of unfit boys for the 'Clerical Examination' with its very large percentage of failures."[26] This reveals the caliber of people who found attraction for the ministry of the church and consequently the quality of faith that ensued.

In Onitsha, where the only secondary school level education was provided at Dennis Memorial Grammar School, founded in 1925 and with much serious attention given to staffing, infrastructure, and general funding, it is obvious that the highest priority of missionary education at this time was in the area of teacher training. The only teacher training college was at Awka. The students were of a higher academic level, and generally more mature: there were, as of April 1930, sixty regular students in residence, thirty junior catechists (older men of tried character), and ten divinity students. The staff consisted of three Europeans and two Africans, all with university honors degrees, in addition to other two African certified teachers with the addition of another European teacher in view. The interest also seemed to have grown quite steadily, rising from six residential students in 1923 to sixty in 1939. The purpose of combining the regular students with catechists in training was for the benefit of positive influence from the older men on younger regular students, and since they would eventually work in the same environment of church and school, side by side, this interaction was a helpful prelude to the anticipated collaboration.

While there was no form of specialized professional training in medicine, engineering, or law, one more area of special interest was in the training of women in Women and Girls' Education. The highest-level education for females was at St. Monica's Women Training College, Ogbunike (founded in 1892), but there was a

26. Church Missionary House. "Missionary Education in The Niger Diocese."

rising interest in the special training preparatory to marriage. These were simple short training centers where courses such as Reading, Writing, and very simple Arithmetic, Hygiene, Singing, Religious Knowledge, and Child Welfare were taught.

Tackling the Crisis

A matter of critical importance in this transition in mission policies had to do with the process and criteria for recruitment. Missionary education was no longer in the hands of the missionaries alone, as was the case in the earlier days. Now the government of the colonies was formulating an educational policy and the missionaries were merely partners whose ideas had to fit into what the government had in mind to do. The greater adjustment therefore had to be done by the missionaries themselves. They too had come to admit that they needed to match the expectations of the government with competent hands. It was considered of critical importance to the CMS that the recruitment process must not lose sight of the delicate stage of missionary enterprise in Africa. The CMS General Secretary, in a memorandum to Oldham, expressed his concerns:

> In Africa, where the old heathen religion is facing modern science, the people who are profoundly religious, are hankering for the secret of a new religious life and power sufficiently strong to resist the impact of a purely secular outlook on life, and at the same time a religion that will enable them to assimilate the best in science to their new faith. Because of this we in CMS feel that we must maintain the religious side of our educational work at a very high level, and that it is essential for us to have men who are not only living Christian lives, but who are prepared to share their convictions and their beliefs with others.[27]

This problem—whether to engage those who were personally more interested in the educational aspects of evangelical work than in the evangelical aspect of education—was extensively discussed

27. Oldham, "CMS General Secretary to Oldham," 1.

at a conference in Swansick in April 1931. Before this conference was convened, the situation received a preliminary response by the appointment of Mr. Victor Murray, on secondment from Selly Oaks colleges, being an educationist, to undertake a visit to Nigeria the following year. The primary purpose may be summarized as follows:

1. To assist the newly formed Christian Council of Nigeria, the churches and missions in Nigeria, and the home boards to arrive at a common view regarding the contribution which Christian education was expected to make to the welfare of the people of Nigeria.

2. To ascertain the steps necessary to make this contribution as effective as possible and the relation of a program of Christian education to the intentions and policies of the government.

All these were aimed at establishing Christian education in Nigeria on a very firm foundation. Mr. Murray did a thorough job of analyzing the situation on the ground, and his findings revealed much about the nature of the crisis in missionary education in Nigeria. Addressing the meeting of the Christian Council of Nigeria from April 1–2, 1932, after his tour, he made these preliminary observations which became part of the missionary education policy:

> I have found the situation in Nigeria to be very difficult, and all the more so because in matters of education personal confidence is the only possible basis of successful organization and it is this factor that has been almost entirely lacking. The change over from a Director of Education who took time and trouble to build up a sympathetic understanding with the missions to one who has made haste too quickly, has caused a psychological problem to which I myself can see no immediate solution.[28]

In trying to help the mission organizations to refocus on their main task, and not be distracted by the changing policies and personnel of the government, he asked penetrating questions:

28. Murray, "Statement of Missionary Education Policy," 2.

"We have to consider why we are here at all, why we have schools at all, whether we would come here simply to run schools, and if not, what is the relation of schools to our essential task."[29] He felt these questions were fundamental and even more important than issues of how much money they had in the bank, or the view of the Director of Education.

These developments in policy at the higher levels of the CMS had to be worked out at the diocesan and district levels which were the grassroots, so to speak. In 1936, the work of the missionary supervisor of schools was finally articulated for the Niger Mission: it was to fulfill the aim of making mission schools fully efficient in building up fine, Christian characters who would be alive to the needs of their land and prepared to make valuable contributions toward their country's progress. The missionary supervisor of schools was to accomplish his task along three main lines: routine school inspections, organizing teacher-training courses, and out-of-school personal friendships with teachers and pupils. These roles, especially the last, were to mark him out as being different from the usual Officer of Education in the colonial administration. Indeed, the missionary supervisor was expected to lodge within the school or church premises rather than in a more distant government rest house. He was to be seen as one who came not primarily to report but to help. He could even take up preaching in the churches during weekends, thus fulfilling his role like any other missionary.

The Situation at the Lokoja Confluence Area

How then did the Lokoja Confluence missionary setting relate with these metamorphoses in the missionary education scenario? To appreciate this, we need to recall the fact that missionary education had been as old as the arrival of the missionaries themselves, resulting in the establishment of the first mission school in Northern Nigeria in 1865. In the report of the major CMS Districts in

29. Murray, "Statement of Missionary Education Policy," 3.

the North (for Zaria by Dr. W. R. Miller, for Bida by A. E. Ball, for Mokwa and Kutigi by J. D. Aitken, for Lokoja by J. L. Macintyre, and for the CUMP Panyam, Kabwir stations and Bauchi by T. E. Alvarez) covering the years 1908–1909, it was reported that the school in Lokoja had increased in numbers and efficiency under Mr. D. S. Cole. The new brick school was formally opened in November 1908 and the names on the register had risen to 120. There were reports of greater enthusiasm in the neighboring Bassa country and Kabba district, including the reoccupation of the early mission station of Gbobe and the building of three churches by the Kabba natives themselves, despite opposition from the native and Muslim populations.

The Watney Training School in Kpata

The same report mentioned two training institutions at this time, both of elementary type. The first was the Watney Training School in Kpata within Bassa country for the training of native evangelists possessing only the rudiments of education. These were later sent to some of the churches. Some of the early ones were: A. Aroniyo, E. Esenyi, and R. Sedu who were sent to Gbobe Akabe, and Kporobi, respectively. As of 15th February 1909, the Northern Nigeria Executive Committee held at Lokoja approved the following students for training as 1st- and 2nd-year students at the school: Samuel Gideon from Bassa Country, Momadu Katugwa from Kabba District for 1st year, and Jiya Moses, who was expected from the Panyam station to commence 2nd year.

The second institution was the Kutigi Training Class at Kutigi in the Nupe country for the training of selected boys up to the Pupil teacher standard, who were being groomed to become teachers in mission schools later on. There is evidence that much attention was given to this training school, for at the same meeting (on the recommendation of Mr. Macintyre, the missionary in charge of the Lokoja area at the time), the Executive Committee decided that the time had come for a test examination for candidates to be admitted. They needed to be able to:

1. read from any of the four Gospels in their vernacular;

2. transcribe any passage from the same;

3. show a knowledge of the main facts of our Lord's life.

In their first year of training, their syllabus was to include: Reading and Writing in the vernacular, Arithmetic, including Compound Addition, Bible Stories, Outlines of Christian Doctrines, Islam, Keeping Church Books, Elements of the English Language. According to Crampton, even this laudable effort at the early stages proved premature.[30]

The Infant School at Lokoja

From the 1908–09 reports of the mission stations, comments about Lokoja always concentrated on the performance of the school. The reports were quite positive at this time both about the Trinity School and the Infant Department. Indeed, the total number of names on the register, as earlier noted, was about 120, with four pupil teachers and a girl probationer. The same Northern Nigeria Executive Committee had a record about the Infant School in Lokoja. The meeting also recorded the approval granted for one of the older girls, Amina, in the Freed Slaves Home in Zungeru, to be sent to Lokoja for training for the purpose of helping with the girls in the Infant School. There was also the hope that she would eventually be able to teach in a girls boarding school being planned for Northern Nigeria at a future date.

Even though they were under the Niger Mission, Rev. J. D. Aitken suggested alterations to the Onitsha Code and Schedules, "making them more adapted to requirements in N. Nigeria."[31] This too received the blessing of the Executive Committee, with the secretary being instructed to "get it working in each District with as little delay as possible."[32]

---

30. Crampton (2004), *Christianity in Northern Nigeria*, 102.

31. Northern Nigeria Executive Committee, Feb. 1909, 21.

32. CMS Northern Nigeria Executive Committee Meeting, 21.

While the desirability of a Secondary Training Center and a Girls' Boarding School in Northern Nigeria was discussed, these sentiments were expressed, and Lokoja was considered to be a favorable location:

> Already the mission was feeling very seriously the need of Christian trained girls as wives for converts and future agents of the mission. There was a nucleus of five Hausa speaking girls from N. Nigeria at Ibadan, available for such a scheme, and if, as seemed most desirable such a school were started in or near Lokoja there would be a possibility of returns from Industrial work, such as baking, and laundry work. There would probably be several other girls ready to come to the school on payment of fees ... and a permanent staff of two European ladies."[33]

Even though the only full-time primary school at this time was the Holy Trinity School at Lokoja, the reports from the districts continued to show much activity in the different levels of educational institutions. Notable among the CMS missionaries who worked in the area at this time was Mr. Thomas E. Alvarez, who became secretary of the Northern Nigeria Mission, residing at Lokoja. From there he traveled extensively to Kabba (eventually taken over in 1924 by the Yoruba Mission), Bassa and Nupe Districts, showing himself an able administrator and great missionary statesman. He continued till 1926 when the European Superintendency was withdrawn in pursuance of the indigenous church policy and Rev. W. A. Thompson, a West Indian who had been involved in the work for a considerable time in Lokoja, took over leadership.

By the late 1930s to the early 1940s, the reports about the school in Lokoja and the ones across the river in Bassa District were quite negative. Even though the tone of Thomas Alvarez appeared more optimistic than that of Miss Ritsert, it was unmistakable that there were some unhappy situations at this time. In his report of 1936–1937, Alvarez expressed the opinion that the two schools at Kpata and Akabe needed to be put on a higher level

---

33. CMS Northern Nigeria Executive Committee Meeting, 22.

since they were already performing satisfactorily with the addition of Standard V. There was even a Brides-to-be class in Kpata under Miss Matthews, but later transferred to Akabe—a mission settlement under Miss Katerine Ritsert.

The role of missionary education and the subsequent involvement of the colonial government had far-reaching implications that shaped the religious, political, economic, and general social climate of the country, for the elite that became the earliest nationalists and founding fathers of Nigerian politics also took their root from these beginnings.

Agents Training Class at Amewa

Even though the Watney Training Centre was considered premature in the first decade of the twentieth century, there is evidence that the idea was revisited yet again, this time at a location called Amewa, about five miles east of the confluence. In the Lokoja- Bassa report for October 1, 1938—March 20, 1939, the superintendent wrote, "I was able in November last to pay a happy visit (3 days) to the evangelist students (sic) at Amewa and their instructor Solomon A. Mama. The second eight students were just completing their year's course."[34] However, by May 1940, the report written by Alfred W. Smith, bishop and superintendent for the same district, indicated the discontinuation of this institution due to lack of funds.

---

34. "Lokoja-Bassa District Report, Oct. 1st 1938—Mar. 20th '39", 1.

Chapter 4

THE PREPARANDI *and* MEDICAL MISSION

(1882–1890)

The Preparandi as the Missionary Training Institution

ONE OF THE INSTITUTIONS OF the CMS that could have been their most enduring legacy in Lokoja, and indeed the educational history of present-day Nigeria was the Preparandi. As the activities of the CMS became consolidated around the confluence communities of the Niger Mission, strategies were worked out to ensure capacity-building and sustainability of the encounter in a setting that was pluralistic, a confluence of different worldviews—both cultural and religious.

As the limitations of the native agents became apparent, and as they were being used against them, it became imperative to take remedial measures. One of those was the establishment of the Preparandi. In CMS engagement around the world, this was a veritable institution in missionary enterprise in the CMS stations. Among the active Preparandi institutions were the ones in South India,

Nagasaki in Japan, and Jerusalem in Palestine. Indeed, the report about the missionary work in the Middle East shows how pivotal such training was to the work of the CMS: "The chief educational institutions maintained by CMS were the Preparandi Institution and Bishop Gobat's School in Jerusalem; a girls' boarding school with teacher training at Bethlehem; an orphanage at Nazareth; the Jerusalem Girls' College and some forty-eight elementary schools, of which the largest was at Gaza".[1]

For a long time after the arrival of the CMS, the staff of the Mission in West Africa was recruited from Sierra Leone. The catechists and church agents came from there. Andrew Walls points out that,

> to a greater extent than has been commonly realized, it provided the labor force: a hundred or more ministers and missionaries in forty years for the CMS alone, and a very much larger number of schoolmasters, catechists, and artisans in mission service who might also do some teaching and preaching . . . Such missionaries reflected the values of Sierra Leone, and when they set up a training institution hundreds of miles up the Niger, they called it *Institution Cauda Preparandi*.[2]

Even those who did not end up being ordained served as clerks, railway men, mechanics, and traders, pervading everywhere that the British influence was found in West Africa. They also became the footmen for the mission, for they took along their Bibles, prayer and hymn books, and the practice of the Christian faith as they had learnt it. Yet, for a good number of them, their taste went beyond the financial capabilities of the mission in comparison with what was obtainable with the secular jobs. The missionary encounter was perceived as a three-pronged affair: Christianity, commerce, and civilization. Bishop Ajayi Crowther preferred the middle-aged ones who didn't have great learning in English and the local languages to flaunt:

1. CMS Archive, 1880–1934.
2. Walls, *Cross-Cultural Process*, 105.

He made periodic analyses in 1868, in 1870 and again in 1877 of the qualifications and merits of his missionary staff, and on each occasion he came to the conclusion that he depended most on middle-aged men barely literate in English and in the vernacular, farmers, carpenters, mechanics, masons, court messengers, stewards on ships and the like by profession, recommended by the Niger Mission Committee in Sierra Leone as men of proven Christian character.[3]

There was also the important observation that they commanded more respect with the traditional rulers than the young, inexperienced men who flaunted their academic qualifications. Besides, even when the highly educated Henry Johnson was sent to Lokoja it appeared to be a punitive measure, as fall-out from the false charges made against him to the home office. He himself let Hutchinson know that he was not being given a fair trial. B. C. Akinpelu Johnson points out that he proceeded on that assignment with the "distinct conviction that he no longer enjoyed the Committee's confidence. He was to be based in Lokoja alone where he knew neither the language nor customs."[4] For him this was a demotion because he felt he would have been capable of doing much more had he been left in Lagos.

By November 1879, further restructuring of the Niger Mission was proposed which was to divide the Mission into two sections, to be known as the "Sudan and the Upper Niger" and the "Delta and the Lower Niger" Missions, respectively. The Sudan and Upper Niger Mission, with Lokoja as its headquarters, would focus on missions to the Muslim communities in those parts, for whom the Hausa and Nupe languages would be required, and would also include the tribes speaking Igbira, the language spoken in the districts around Gbobe northwards.

Being cash-strapped and frequently tasked by a dearth of competent staff was a besetting challenge for Bishop Crowther in his daunting assignment. Worse still, this was further compounded

---

3. Ade-Ajayi, *Christian Missions,* 222.

4. Johnson, *Me and My House,* 85.

by the unsettling reports being sent to the home office about his staff. This created the urgent need for the release of funds for setting up a training institution in Lokoja—the Preparandi in 1883. It took another four years for the building to be completed, while all this time the ministry continued to grow at a fast tempo beyond what a new institution could possibly handle.

It is inevitable that the building of the Preparandi in Lokoja should be posited in the context of the build-up to the Niger Mission crisis, a time when the moral and intellectual lapses of the native workers—both actual scandals and some mischievously contrived—were played up to justify the rising racial innuendoes.

The opening of the Preparandi was reported in the CMS Intelligencer of January 1888 under the reports about the Mission Field in West Africa, "On Sept. 21st, the *Preparandi* Institution at Lokoja was formally opened with a special service and addresses by the Bishop and Archdeacons Hamilton and Johnson."[5] The first six students were Igbos. Crowther's biographer, Jesse Page, saw this initiative as a new dawn in the missionary enterprise:

> In reviewing the work of the Mission on the Niger, the practical mind of Bishop Crowther is stamped on everything. In dealing with native races the spiritual must be allied to the educational, and especially where the wise course is being adopted of preparing the converts themselves for work among their own people. The foolish but prevalent idea, that the African intelligence cannot develop under teaching, is at once exploded by the spectacle of such a work as is carried on at the Preparandi Institution at Lokoja, situated at the confluence of the Binue and Niger. This was started by the Bishop for the further training of native boys as catechists and school-masters. The stones to erect this substantial building were collected from the hills around, and the 15,000 pieces were carried by women to the mason who had been specially sent from Sierra Leone for the purpose of the work. Everything was paid for, and the sight of a number of men and women engaged in industry, properly remunerated,

5. Hamilton, "West Africa," 4.

was a significant feature of that district. The place is a perfect marvel to the natives. They cannot understand how the stones keep together for such a height; and as they look in wonder, say to each other, "White man pass every man; white man, he next to God." It is quite on the College plan, with tutors' residences, dormitories, classrooms, and a printing room, the gift of the Society for Promoting Christian Knowledge. Such a center of spiritual and educational activity will influence to an untold extent the future of the West Coast of Africa.[6]

Fatusi, also looking at it from the viewpoint of the products of the institution even at the early stages, sees it as a mark of Crowther's ingenuity that was hopeful for the mission: From its inception in 1883, it catered to six students, all Igbo from Onitsha, who graduated in 1887, five qualifying as teachers and preachers employed to the south of the confluence, with one of them a printer. By that year, also, a new batch of six students was admitted. The institution was, thus, a vital element for missionary and educational expansion, and an early start in promoting technological instruction and producing technical manpower.[7]

But the Sudan Party—that group of young, overzealous missionaries, led by Graham Wilmot Brooke (aged 25), a freelance lay missionary, and J. Alfred Robinson—saw things differently. As Ade-Ajayi notes,

> When these missionaries arrived at Lokoja in 1889 and saw the building of the Preparandi Institution, a two-story house which was completed in 1887, built by the European catechist John Burness to Archdeacon Henry Johnson's specifications, they declared it to be the grandest building in West Africa and an obstacle to the progress of Christianity . . . They said that Henry Johnson must have deceived the Parent Committee about its real size, charged him with, among other things, being extravagant and asked for him to be removed to Sierra Leone. They sold the building at once to the Royal Niger

6. Page and Crowther, *Slave Boy,* 145–46.

7. Fatusi, "Retransmission," 153.

Company at the company's price, without waiting for the decision of the Parent Committee on the wisdom of the step.[8]

Ade-Ajayi further notes that the bishop was completely left out of the negotiations with the Royal Niger Company (RNC). The brand new Preparandi Training Institute was sold for £1,500 "in exchange for a more modest building for £650 to be used as a Hospital and the remaining £850 in cash for the use of the Sudan Mission. The RNC turned the Preparandi into Army barracks"[9] This was indeed a project coming at a time described as "The end of an Era"[10] by Felix Ekechi when the European colleagues had become overlords as they had no confidence in the native agency staff. At a conference held in Madeira in 1881, the unfortunate decision was taken to dismiss most of the African missionaries on the claim that they didn't live up to the ideals of the Christian faith. Even Bishop Ajayi Crowther's powers were considerably stripped. Archdeacon Henry Johnson was removed from Lokoja to Lagos, and his capable assistant, Rev. C. Paul, who had put in 25 years of faithful service, was moved to the Lower Niger pending issues they could use as a basis for his eventual removal. The students and teachers of the Preparandi were dismissed.[11]

Crampton rightly notes the serious consequences of this sad turn of events in his comments: "It is difficult to assess the effect of this tension upon the evangelization of the area, but in all probability the restriction of the work of the African missionaries retarded the work to such a degree that in places it has never recovered."[12] The membership of the communicants in Lokoja went on a downward spiral. Even the friendly Muslim monarchs like the Emir of Bida became hostile to the presence of white missionaries who had so treated their tested and trusted native agents so disdainfully.

8. Ade-Ajayi, *Christian Missions*, 251.

9. Falola, *Tradition and Change in Africa*, 116.

10. Ekechi, *Missionary Enterprise*, 57.

11. Falola, *Tradition and Change in Africa*, 116.

12. Crampton, *Christianity in Northern Nigeria*, 29.

The CMS Medical Mission

As the terrain of missionary engagement became increasingly bumpy, other initiatives came to the fore. For a few months in 1882, Dr. Percy Brown had carried on medical missionary work at Lokoja at the Society's house on Mount Stirling, which attracted many people from near and far. But death took him away quite early, for Eugene Stock records that "the Society planned a medical mission at Lokoja, and sent out a young doctor, Percy Brown; but he fell sick, was put on board ship for England, and died on the voyage."[13]

The new arrangement of the mission was to set up a Soudan and Upper Niger Mission, with Wilmot Brooke and Robinson, who were volunteers, in charge. The plan included medical missions as an attraction to the Muslims. The March 1890 edition of the *Church Missionary Intelligencer* records the decision of the committee to appoint Dr. C. F. Harford-Battersby to the task of resuscitating the Medical Mission again at Lokoja. They expressed great hopes in this new venture as their correspondence to Harford-Battersby shows:

> The present proposed extension of the Mission into the Soudan seemed to the Committee a favorable opportunity for re-attempting a Medical Mission, which they believe may have, in a peculiar degree, the effect of softening the prejudices of the Mohammedan community and of bringing them into contact with the Gospel. The re-arrangements in the Mission provide at the very moment, in the large building known as the "Preparandi Institution," vacated by the Archdeacon consequent on Lokoja having been constituted the base of the Soudan and Upper Niger Mission under the new scheme, a building ready to hand and admirably adapted for use as a hospital, and which, not being needed under the altered arrangements for any other purpose, is immediately available for this special use. The Committee also regard it as a providential circumstance that the termination of your own engagement simultaneously with the adoption of these proposals should have allowed you to

13. Stock, *Church Missionary Society*, 3:387.

offer your services, already secured to the Society, for this particular post, to which the Committee have thankfully assigned you.[14]

Even though Dr. Percy Brown's time was brief, his medical work outlived him in the people's memories. Once a native agent, Mr. Williams, was challenged by a local chief during one of their evangelistic journeys around Lokoja, who argued that "the custom of our fathers should be followed." Mr. Williams replied: "When the late white doctor was in Lokoja, everyone from the towns far and near left their Native doctors and brought to him their sick, and he did many of them good. Why were they not satisfied with their Native doctors but accepted the prescriptions of the new and strange doctor?" The other villagers present affirmed loudly, "True, true." This became the opportunity to press home the fact that the gospel was more efficacious than the traditional religion, concluding, "In the same way, all the prescriptions of your former doctors are unavailing to give your souls the cure they need before God. The Word of God, which you do not possess, gives the true and only means of salvation for sinful man, therefore accept this new and only way."[15]

Dr. Harford-Battersby's attestation of the pioneer work of his predecessor was quite positive: "as far as Medical Mission work is concerned in Lokoja, I have only the unblemished record of Dr. Brown's work, which has not been forgotten; Mr. Thomas at Gbebe and a Church member there, who was one of his patients, telling me much of his good work."[16] The new building provided was considered quite suitable.

By 3rd May 1890, medical work had been taken to Gbobe which at the time was said to be bigger than Lokoja, being inhabited mostly by refugees who had fled from the exactions of the Nupe princes in Lokoja. Others came to seek medical assistance from the neighboring communities, such as the Igbiras described as a

14. CMS Intelligencer (March 1890), "Instructions," 177.

15. CMS Intelligencer (March 1890), "Mission Field," 188.

16. CMS Intelligencer (Oct. 1890), "Report of Dr. C.F. Harford-Battersby," 696.

"race inhabiting the waterside towns for about ten miles above and below the confluence, and about ninety miles up the Binue."[17] They also traded with the Bassas described as "emigrants from Nupe, an important little tribe of brave agriculturists who successfully hold a strip of mountain country, east and south-east of Gbebe, against all comers."[18] They were considered "a most promising field for Mission work in the immediate future."[19]

The reports by Dr. Harford-Battersby give a vivid idea of the situation at Gbobe, the confluence station:

> The out-patient work has been very important. By God's wonderful providence I have not been overwhelmed with work, as they do not come to me for every slight ailment, having their own medicines, which someday I hope to investigate. The cases have been chiefly surgical, always the most satisfactory, and from not coming in too great numbers I have had more time for spiritual work, and most of them have had the Gospel presented to them. Among the out-patients I have had strangers from Kano, Sokoto, Bida, Ilorin, and several other places not so far distant, but who collect in this important center. But perhaps the most important work in the Medical Mission here has been the visits to patients in their homes. Everywhere a welcome is found, and even in some of the most influential Mohammedan households a cordial reception is met with.[20]

Over time, the work in Gbobe whittled down, as Lokoja gained more prominence as a rallying point for the growing population of mixed multitudes. The medical missions became more localized in some communities, like the Bassa Country where Akabe became the station for an elementary school, maternity ward, and a boarding facility in the 1930s.

17. CMS Intelligencer (Oct. 1890), "Soudan and Upper Niger Mission," 687.

18. CMS Intelligencer (Oct. 1890), "Soudan and Upper Niger Mission," 687.

19. CMS Intelligencer (Oct. 1890), "Soudan and Upper Niger Mission," 686.

20. CMS Intelligencer (Oct. 1890), "Report of Dr. C.F. Harford-Battersby," 696.

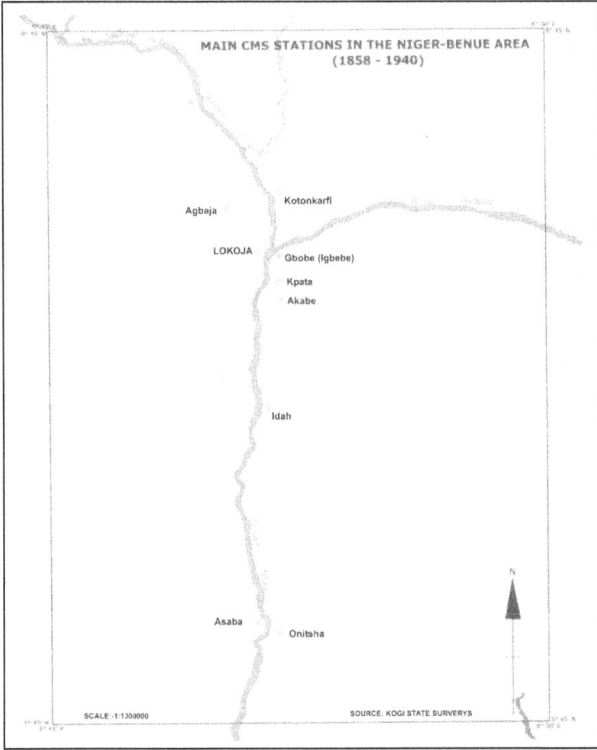

MAIN CMS STATIONS IN THE NIGER-BENUE AREA
(1858 - 1940)

Agbaja
Kotonkarfi
LOKOJA
Gbobe (Igbebe)
Kpata
Akabe
Idah
Asaba
Onitsha

N

SCALE :1:1300000

SOURCE: KOGI STATE SURVERYS

Niger Mission Showing Lokoja Niger Benue Confluence Area

Holy Trinity Primary School, Lokoja, founded 1865, first in northern Nigeria

69

Mission House at Kpata in Bassa Country, built 1933

CMS Maternity at Akabe, Bassa Country, built 1936

Chapter 5

NATIVE AGENCY *in the* NIGER MISSION
(1867–1902)

"Native Agency" conveys the sense of ambiguity by which the Native, even when designated a principal, exercised not his own but only delegated power, and acted not from his own conviction but in dependence on others."

ADE-AJAYI[1]

OVER TIME THE HISTORY OF Christian missions in Africa has thrown up major issues of identity, inculturation, and relevance. While the content of the gospel as the essential agency of conversion remains sacrosanct, the inescapable reality has been the necessity of decking it in native garb. This is the process whereby that which first appeared foreign becomes indigenized, as the continuing incarnation or invasion of the divine into a variety of human contexts. In classic Christian understanding, this is the event of God coming down to earth to take on human flesh and sharing in the experience of humanity.

---

1. Falola, *Tradition and Change in Africa*, 120–21.

Missionary advance has evolved with best practices that are constantly being reviewed and reevaluated in different situations to enable the recipients to go beyond that initial ambiguous identity to that of becoming hosts and owners of the faith. Many factors have either aided or impeded this objective and constrained further initiatives to make the process of transmission meaningful and less threatening. This caution has been sounded repeatedly, and just one instance might do here: "It is [therefore] important, when thinking of African theology, to remember that it will act on an African agenda. It is useless for us to determine what we think an African theology ought to be doing: it will concern itself with questions that worry Africans."[2]

The shape of Christianity that emerges depends largely on the institutional agencies and agents involved. The latter engages our focus in this chapter as we look more closely at Evangelist Thomas Walter Bako, a native agent (catechist) with the CMS in the Lokoja area in the period of his ministry from 1877–1902, when he was martyred.

That period necessarily calls attention to missionary methodology as it affects both the agency and the agents. A brief scan of the landscape shows that this concern is by no means peculiar to the discourse on African Christianity. What looks like a stirring of the hornet's nest that gained considerable attention in mission practice is also highlighted in Roland Allen's *Missionary Methods: St. Paul's or Ours?* According to him,

> Men have wandered over the world, 'preaching the Word,' laying no solid foundations, establishing nothing permanent, leaving no really instructed society behind them, and have claimed St. Paul's authority for their absurdities. They have gone through the world, spending their time in denouncing ancient religions, in the name of St. Paul. They have wandered from place to place without any plan or method of any kind, guided in their movements by straws and shadows, persuaded they were imitating St. Paul on his journey from Antioch to Troas.

2. Walls, *Missionary Movement*, 11.

Almost every intolerable abuse that has ever been known in the mission field has claimed some sentence or act of St. Paul as its original.[3]

The fundamental nature of this concern is seen by its dominance in discussions on African Christianity. Donovan, after seventeen years of work among the Masai in Tanzania, observes that "a missionary must respect the culture of a people, not destroy it. The incarnation of the gospel, the flesh and blood which must grow on the gospel, is up to the people of a culture."[4]

The Necessity of Native Agency

The "Native Agents" were the interpreters of two worldviews—the Christian and the Native. African native agents were undoubtedly a great asset in the task of propagating Christian faith and values. They were sometimes the unsung heroes who did the pioneering spade work of the missionary enterprise, sometimes doubling as educationists, or health workers, thus becoming the firstfruits of Henry Venn's ideal of the "euthanasia of the mission."[5] A common and erroneous assumption is that they were essentially the uneducated (and, therefore, unintelligent) category. However, there were, among them, icons and elites, as well as the less educated, and those better suited to the local environment, given the tribal variations that were not obvious to the foreign missionaries who assumed that every African was suited to every African community.

In the Nigerian experience of missionary encounter, there were three main areas where they touched during those initial efforts: the coastal cities like "Badagri and Lagos to the west, Calabar, Bonny and Brass to the east; . . . secondly, the interior of the Yoruba country, especially Abeokuta, Ibadan, Ijaye, Oyo; . . . and

3. Allen, *Missionary Methods,* 5.

4. Donovan, *Christianity Rediscovered,* 30.

5. Shenk, *Henry Venn,* 118–25.

thirdly, the Niger Valley, especially Onitsha, Aboh, Idah, Lokoja and Egga."[6]

Several factors favored the engagement of native agents. Slavery was still thriving in the interior of Africa even though it had been abolished by the British Parliament. It was necessary to introduce legitimate trade as part of a multidimensional approach to tackle the menace of the yet-thriving, evil trade.

The Returnees: Liberated Slaves

In the first category were the liberated slaves who had become converted to Christianity in Sierra Leone, and then nursed a yearning to return to their native lands. Some of them were artisans and craftsmen. Besides the joy of reunion with their relatives, they were the trusted hands to both the foreign missionaries, as well as their communities. Certainly, such a dual role had its thrills and ills, for they often found themselves in the awkward position of being allies to the one, and renegades to the other. The expressed conviction by the likes of Sir Fowell Buxton that these liberated slaves were God's chosen instruments for the redemption of their fellow Africans was a great motivation for them. As an evangelical and a leader of the anti-slavery movement he wrote a book, *The African Slave Trade and Its Remedy,* in which he proposed that liberated Africans be educated and made part of this new venture: "we must elevate the minds of her people and call forth the resources of her soil," predicting that this would result in a flourishing of the agricultural enterprise, legitimate trade, civilization, and Christianity.[7]

To circumvent the monopoly of the coastal chiefs who still controlled the slave trade, and because of the harsh weather conditions which posed fatal dangers to the European missionaries, he proposed that Africans liberated from Sierra Leone and the Americas would be the most suitable agents. Besides their other engagements, Ajayi captures his optimism that,

6. Ade-Ajayi, *Christian Missions,* xiv.

7. Buxton, *African Slave Trade,* 282.

As catechists and schoolmasters, they would preach Christianity; as carpenters, tailors, sawyers, masons and artisans, they would improve the standard of housing and household furniture and build the necessary roads and bridges to make a highway for legitimate trade. They would be commercial agents to encourage the cultivation of crops like cotton and indigo . . . They would teach new arts and new ideas and in every way bring down the old society on which the slave trade was based and set up in its place a new social order.[8]

They indeed became the middlemen among the merchants, for they were armed with the Christian worldview in addition to that in which they were raised.

Home-grown Agents

But there was also a second category of native agents: those who were never sold into slavery but who, though rooted in their communities, were attracted to the English way of life and the new faith that was preached, and so became the firstfruits, the early converts, and pupils. They were the ones who were employed as stewards and staff of the mission. Their training and maturity had a bearing on how much they were able to contribute to the mission outlook. Even if some of these workers were not the first choice of the mission administrators, the paucity of funds constrained the mission to engage these local hands who were affordable. Unfortunately, what was gained in economic terms was forfeited in other ways more critical to the mission, as the Niger Mission crisis proved; for some of the local agents had serious moral lapses that put the reputation of the entire missionary enterprise in jeopardy.

The Elite Category of Indigenous Agents

There were also those who could easily be categorized as the elite category of indigenous missionaries, the highly trained ones such

8. Ade-Ajayi, *Christian Missions*, 11.

as Bishop Crowther, and his son, Dandeson; Rev. (later Bishop) James Johnson, also known as Holy Johnson; Archdeacon Henry Johnson and the Rev. J. Boyle. They were in a position to project and uphold values that were critical to the integrity and sustainability of the mission beyond the storms that threatened to engulf the Niger Mission. Knowing the importance of cultivating respectable relationships with those in authority in the communities they tried to evangelize, Crowther ensured mutual respect for every ruler they encountered, opting more for reformation of old customs rather than outright denunciation and uprooting as his foreign counterparts sometimes did. As Ajayi notes, "he came to regard the ability to work with local rulers for the reform of the old town as the most essential training for a missionary."[9]

Respect for African Customs

These native agents interpreted the new faith to their fellow natives, and interpreted their cultural values to the foreign missionaries, thus averting unnecessary conflicts and crisis. This accords with the community orientation of African societies and the disposition of these native agents toward peaceful coexistence. Their understanding of spirituality was not limited to the narrow confines of church membership, attendance, and liturgy, but extended to relationships within the larger society—including peaceful coexistence, rather than confrontation. In his charge of 1869, Bishop Crowther told his clergy that

> Christianity does not undertake to destroy national assimilation; where there are any degrading and superstitious defects, it corrects them; where they are connected with politics, such corrections should be introduced with due caution and with all meekness of wisdom, that there may be good and perfect understanding between us and the powers that be . . . Their native Mutual Aid Clubs should not be despised, but where there is any with superstitious connections, it should be corrected

9. Ade-Ajayi, *Christian Missions,* 221.

and improved after a Christian model. Amusements are acknowledged on all hands to tend to relieve the mind and sharpen the intellect. If any such is not immoral or indecent, tending to corrupt the mind, but merely an innocent play for amusement, it should not be checked because of its being native and of a heathen origin. Of these kinds of amusements are fables, story-telling, proverbs and songs which may be regarded as stores of their national education in which they exercise their power of thinking . . . their religious terms and ceremonies should be carefully observed; the wrong use made of such terms does not depreciate their real value, but renders them more valid when we adopt them in expressing Scriptural terms in their right senses and places from which they have been applied for want of better knowledge.[10]

Available records attest to the positive outcome of this conciliatory posture of the revered native bishop:

By 1870 Bishop Crowther and his African lieutenants had succeeded in overcoming the suspicion of the traditional rulers, that they were heralds of alien rule. These missionaries carried out their activity within customary laws and traditional politics; they recognized and respected the authority of the chiefs and courted their favor and influence for the progress of their enterprises; there was no question of bluffing or hectoring. Patience, amiableness, sympathy and forbearance were their watchword.[11]

Indeed, Bishop Crowther earned the reputation of being the most trusted foreign influence in Nupe Kingdom, whose counsel was courted with much regard. When the British consulate at Lokoja was abandoned in 1887, Bishop Crowther was the trusted person to recommend Jacob Mehieux Musa, a liberated Muslim native convert to administer Lokoja, and draw up the constitution.

James Johnson insisted that every African who had proven ability should be accorded appropriate respect. He advocated a reform of the Anglican liturgy when he listened to an *Ifa* priest who

10. Crowther, *Charge Delivered on the Banks,* CA3/04.

11. Ayandele, "Missionary Factor," 1.

had become a Christian convert talk so exultingly about the attributes of God, feeling there was much that was instructive about presenting the Christian God to the heathen. He spoke against and sought reformation of the exclusivist practice of separating the Mission House from the host community, which, according to him,

> made the Christian to be regarded as a people separate from the community, as identifying themselves with a foreign people: the dress they usually assume has become a badge of distinction: the distance between them and the heathens is far greater than that between heathens and Mohammedans. Often many heathens and Mohammedans are found living together in the same house. Christians are rarely found living thus with either.[12]

The practice in the Upper Niger Mission was a combination of political tact and missionary diplomacy as they chose their missionary locations. For instance, Rev. Charles Paul, who was in charge of the Kippo Hill station—the northernmost CMS Niger mission—ensured that their station was removed from the important trade routes that were vulnerable to Islamic influence. He opted more for the serene location which he equated as a demonstration of the divine nature of their missionary work. It soon attracted attention for other reasons, principally as a refuge for those who fled the exactions and high-handedness of the Nupe rulership at different times. There were rules for those they allowed into the station: they were to attend the services on Sundays and should not be polygamists. But also, the design of their buildings and general outlook of the mission environment was to be, according to Kolapo, "a demonstration both of Christianity and of civilization."[13] He further notes that, at Lokoja, the Rev. T. C. John ensured architectural affinity in all their buildings, with the taste of the parent community. But what means one thing to one party means entirely something else to another—especially when looking at the host community. At the Niger-Benue Confluence, as

12. J. Johnson to Hutchinson, 6 March 1876; CMS CA2/056.

13. Kolapo, *Christian Missionary Engagement*, 108.

in a number of other stations, the missionaries were allocated the parcels of land that were considered the abode of the evil spirits. Kolapo cites some instances:

> At Lokoja, at the Confluence of the Niger and Benue, the CMS missionary party were involved in cutting down some trees locally held to be sacred to make room for their own buildings and James Thomas was once approached by a local chief to join other local farmers in contributing money and material to propitiate one such tree to ensure good rain during the cropping season.[14]

This has an interesting resonance with the observation Fretheim makes about the practice of the Basel Mission to separate the Christian communities ("salems") from the host communities. Even though the introduction of Jamaican missionaries had brought more credibility and strengthened the view that one could be both African and Christian, this practice was virtually counterproductive. Citing a case of Akropong, she makes the point that,

> the Christians occupied a part of the town with buildings and houses built for Riis . . . This in part fostered the troubling belief that to become Christian meant a clear separation, and in many instances rejection of one's culture, religion, and non-Christian community. Furthermore, it inculcated the view that Christianity was a foreign religion, one that required adherents to leave their communities and adapt their lifestyles to the pietistic ideal of Christian communal living.[15]

All these communicated the impression that the Christian faith led ultimately to an alienation from the host culture, and those who embraced it were considered renegades. For some people, it was too much a price to pay for their embracing a new faith which jeopardized their privileges, which in some cases were royal.

---

14. Kolapo, *Christian Missionary Engagement*, 89.
15. Fretheim, *Kwame Bediako*, 63.

The African Indigenous Agents in the Marketplace

It is important to highlight the role of the others who were not necessarily on the staff of the missions, but who saw themselves as stakeholders in the new faith and its accompanying interests. Of course, they maintained active church membership in various denominations. They became vocal in the face of the insinuations arising from the Niger Mission crisis:

> Of the 41 signatories to the memorandum from the Lagos community in October 1890 to protest to the CMS on the treatment meted out to Bishop Crowther and his staff on the Niger, 8 were Ministers—5 from the CMS, one Baptist, and 2 Methodists; 10 were senior government officials—2 medical doctors, the sub-Inspector of Schools, the Chief Registrar of the Supreme Court and his deputy, the Postmaster, the Chief Statistician of the Customs and his Assistant, the Keeper of the Powder Magazine, and the Chief Clerk in the Governor's Office. All these were Native Agents and once it was agreed that the Bishop, the most outstanding example of Native Agency, had failed, none of them had the chance during the colonial period to be succeeded in comparable positions of authority by fellow Africans.[16]

The sense of solidarity against what they perceived to be imperialistic high-handedness, even in mission circles, showed the value of community support that was strong among these native workers across all vocations.

The Ministry of Thomas Walter Bako
(CMS Agent, c1877—June 2, 1902)

Philip Jenkins observes that, "For any missionary venture, the ordination of native clergy must be the acid test of commitment

---

16. Ade-Ajayi, *Patriot to the Core*, 122.

to moving beyond an imperial context, to leaving the veranda."[17] Engaging native hands was a necessity as well as a risk.

Thomas Walter Bako was not the most outstanding indigenous worker. There were others, but he became the one to pay the supreme price, while engaged in ministry within Lokoja, his homeplace. He became the first recorded Christian martyr in northern Nigeria, after Joshua Hart of Bonny in the Niger Delta area. He was one of the native agents with the CMS in the Lokoja Niger-Benue Confluence area, which was then known as the Upper Niger Mission.

Besides the accounts found in the *Christian Missionary Intelligencer*, another relevant source in recovering his profile is the biography of his grandson, the Rt. Rev. George Bako, who became the pioneer Anglican Bishop of Lokoja Diocese, within the area where he had been martyred.

Thomas Walter Bako was to be sold as a slave at the age of six before he was rescued by the Rev. T. C. John, a CMS worker in Lokoja in the 1880s. The said biography has this account: "He received his education in Lokoja and, in 1887, he was sent to the CMS Training Institution run by the Rev. C. A. Gollmer in Lagos."[18]

While in Lagos, he met Deborah, also a rescued slave girl, who was from the Lokoja area. She was living with the Rev. and Mrs. Gollmer. A relationship developed which blossomed into marriage. The said biography continues,

> On completion of his training in Lagos, Thomas Bako was sent back to work in the Niger area where he spent some years in the Kipo Hill station until 1886 when he was transferred back to Lokoja. Thomas was with the Bishop Ajayi Crowther on the Niger Mission. He was also with Bishop Tugwell and others during their visit to Zaria and Kano.[19]

About this time, he applied to be considered for ordination into Holy Orders, and received a favorable recommendation by

17. Jenkins, *Next Christendom*, 37.
18. Ezebube, *George Bako*, 75.
19. Ezebube, *George Bako*, 75.

the Rev. T. Robinson, who remarked that he was "A very faithful servant of the society for many years and all of us here rejoice to think he may be admitted to the Holy Orders in due course."

Six years passed and the "due course" had not materialized. He, like his fellow native agents, James Thomas Ikubaje and Edward Cline, continued with much passion in their assigned evangelistic duties in the flourishing CMS mission station at Gbobe, as well as the other locations of their itineration. The journal of a fellow missionary, Mr. E. A. J. Thomas, about one of their itinerant evangelistic outings in the Lokoja area, reveals him as a man of much zeal and commitment to the task of evangelizing his "benighted people" (to use a favorite phrase of Ikubaje). These journal entries for some days in February 1898, which were later reported in the *Church Missionary Intelligencer* of August that year, show this catechist in action, providing valuable insight into his personality:

> Feb, 9th, 1898
>
> The nights are very cold, owing to the Harmattan. I slept in a canoe, the rest on a sandbank. Mosquitoes and sandflies are terrible! Reached Adama, a village on the bank. The people were rather frightened at first; about sixty came afterwards. Palm-trees to be seen (there are no palms in Lokoja); very pretty. Reached Keya at 10.30; it is built under a steep hill. Being market day there were many people. We preached in the chief's *katamba* (or reception house). The noise, dust, and beat were such that the preachers there were nearly choked. Dakaki spoke to the chief and people in a fine *katamba* built of mud and wattle, with walls twenty feet high, and lids of English china let into the mud. The chief sat on a raised throne, . . . He seemed amused when I said I wanted women and children to hear as well as the men; the women had to sit outside, and all listened well as we told the "Glad Tidings," and they repeated the little prayer, *"Isa Almasihu egi Soko bomiya"* ("Jesus Christ the Son of God, save me"), Mr. Bako carefully explaining what the words meant.[20]

20. Thomas, "Preaching Christ on the Upper Niger," 584.

On yet another day, 13th February, he records that "all to hear my message he came outside, and we had a good gathering. . . . Mr. Bako is a great help to me."[21]

Missionary after missionary testified to his diligence and effectiveness, especially in communicating the gospel to them in their native language. He was always the bridge between the foreign missionaries and the natives. Another account presents the scenario vividly:

> We were the first white men to visit, and the first Christians to preach in this village, so that they were absolutely raw Heathen, only meeting other people when their women went to market, we felt it a great privilege to speak to them. Mr. Bako, in conclusion, gave them a good straight talk; and they listened with rapt attention the whole time he was speaking. It was difficult to keep silence with an audience like that. On every side dark faces, and yet still darker hearts drinking in for the first time the everlasting Gospel. We left them, but it was with a peculiar joy in our hearts, as we thought that perhaps God, by His grace, had enabled us to help them to take a first step out of heathen darkness into the glorious light and liberty of the Gospel[22]

About four years later, at the end of May 1902, he was on another evangelistic outreach to develop new stations in the Koton Karfe and Umaisha areas, accompanied by Ogbegha and two schoolboys. While returning late, according to Isichei, "he had been told that the road was unsafe but thought that since he had only food and bedding with him, no one would trouble him. He was attacked by robbers and shot with a poisoned arrow"[23] at Tawari, near Koton Karfe, some distance from Lokoja on 3rd June 1902. The account presented by Aitken (dated June 5th 1902) in the *Intelligencer* is quite vivid:

21. Thomas, "Preaching Christ on the Upper Niger," 586.

22. Aitken, "Mission Field," 611.

23. Isichei, *Varieties of Christian Experience*, 72.

Bako was shot through the muscle of the thigh just above the knee-joint, so preventing his running away. Ogbegha then ran into the bush and so escaped, whilst Bako told the boys in Nupe how and where to run away . . . The robbers then attacked Mr. Bako with swords and gave him some terrible wounds, when he fell down and feigned death, whilst they beat him with sticks and, stripping him of most of his clothes, left him for dead . . . Bako was left in the bush for a night, and kept some wild animals away by coughing, his wounds preventing him from doing anything else. Next day the chief of Umaisha sent a chief man and bearers to bring Bako in, tended him until I brought him to Lokoja, where after paddling half the night, we arrived next morning. Blood-poisoning had, however, already set in, and three days after he died, after a night of great suffering.[24]

Isichei further comments that, even though his death was due to the attack of robbers rather than outright opposition to the Christian faith, it was nonetheless martyrdom: "He was not a martyr in the same sense as Joshua Hart, who deliberately chose death rather than deny Christ. But he consciously chose a dangerous road in his endeavor to spread the Gospel; his death was the direct consequence of his missionary work."[25]

As it turned out, his own son, J. A. Bako, became an Anglican clergyman—the position which he sought for himself but never attained. The records reveal that, even though his supervisors had thought very highly of him, and recommended him accordingly, this denial was more a factor of the racism of the white missionaries, which was at its peak in the CMS Niger Mission at this time.[26] By this time, Mr. E. A. J. Thomas, with whom he had gone round the villages some years earlier and who had found him so helpful, had been reassigned to Sintu in West China. When he got this tragic news, he sent this tribute:

24. Aitken, "Mission Field," 612.

25. Isichei, *Varieties of Christian Experience in Nigeria*, 71

26. Isichei, *Varieties of Christian Experience in Nigeria*, 71.

I really learnt to love and respect him more than any of my native brethren, he was so humble, so earnest, so thoughtful. He nursed me once with the gentleness of a woman when fever had brought me down almost to "the Valley of the Shadow" . . . During several itinerations Mr. Bako was my helper, and nothing ever came amiss; he worked hard, whether in preaching or in pacifying unruly carriers. At night we read God's Word together and prayed.[27]

He went on to disclose how Mr. Bako, in the year 1899, refused very tempting offers by Lt. Col. Pilcher, who was then in command at Lokoja, to leave the CMS and accept a post under the colonial government. He was clearly the man for the hour. As a sign of the continuing reverence accorded to his memory, one of his grandsons, Christopher A. S. H. Bako has been offered a traditional in the Lokoja traditional Council, which is the leadership group that advises the traditional ruler.

We may surmise that these indigenous missionary agents, and in particular, Thomas Walter Bako, brought into the identity of Christianity a high level of credibility in their setting, proving that native converts could be genuinely committed to the Christian faith. There was a sense of community responsibility and support for each other. This came out in the approach of Bishop Crowther and his staff as they sought to preserve or christianize values that appeared to be in conflict for reasons of ignorance. This enriched the faith as it took root in the African landscape and cultural milieu. They believed Africa had something to offer.

James Johnson's approach, earlier cited, is equally relevant in this respect. That Thomas Bako was willing to take risks for the sake of propagating the gospel recalls Christ's own approach as he prepared to die for those he came to save, even when his disciples tried to dissuade him; or even the apostle Paul, who said to those who warned him that danger was ahead, "What are you doing, weeping and breaking my heart? For I am ready not only to be

---

27. CMS *Intelligencer*, Feb. 1903, 121.

imprisoned but even to die in Jerusalem for the name of the Lord Jesus."[28]

Their exposure to the two worldviews of their native culture and Christianity made them trusted interpreters who indeed redeemed and enriched both perspectives.

In a setting that was almost always rooted in orality, some of the prayers and songs were indicative of how far Christianity had taken root. When, in one of the villages, the women prayed that Jesus should save them, there was more than spiritual salvation in view, for the African spiritual worldview includes manipulative negative forces that required exorcism and deliverance that was more akin to the setting of Christ's own ministry than that of the Western missionaries. Indeed, this confession by William D. Taylor, Executive Director of Missions Commission of World Evangelical Alliance, in 2003 could hold true for many foreign missionaries:

> I wish I had known and embraced a practicing supernaturalism that would have enabled me to confront a reality close to the experience of Jesus and the early church. During those seventeen years I had occasion to confront the evil one in diverse situations. But I had neither a theology nor ministry skills to adequately deal with evil supernaturalism. My theological paradigm of those years explained away too much or labelled it as superstition. I cannot rewind history and start again, but perhaps others can learn from my experience.[29]

Some observations and conclusions are apparent however one views the involvement of the indigenous agents. Ade-Ajayi takes a swipe at the intentions of the native agency when he opines that,

> "Native Agency" conveys the sense of ambiguity by which the Native, even when designated a principal, exercised not his own but only delegated power, and acted not from his own conviction but in dependence on

28. Acts 21:13.
29. Taylor, "Greatest Personal Lessons," 317.

others. Crowther always knew that he was on trial and he always prayed that he should not fail as that would block the way for others following after him.[30]

In more ways than are obvious, there was immeasurable benefit by the inclusion and participation of the native agents in the propagation of the Christian faith. Sanneh endorses their role, and gives them due credit:

> The local agents rose to the challenge and took charge of the direction that mother tongue deployment indicated for Christianity and for their societies. An inculturated Christianity is not merely a sequel of discredited versions of the religion; it anticipates an emancipated society, a situation for which local leadership is best suited.[31]

What could be considered a major advocacy for the native agency is found when he writes

> [t]he degree to which Christianity became integrated into a particular culture was a useful means of assessing the success of Christian preaching. But it was also a means of determining the level of compromise. Once an entire culture opened itself to the Christian presence it was possible for the missionary to influence and mold that culture without fear of total rejection.[32]

---

30. Falola, *Tradition and Change in Africa*, 20–21.

31. Sanneh, *Whose Religion?*, 25.

32. Sanneh, *Whose Religion?*, 37.

Bishop Crowther and his native Clergy
(Source: Jesse Page, *The Black Bishop*, p. 291)

The Pioneer mission party to Hausaland
(Source: Miller, *Reflections of a Pioneer*, 1936)

Chapter 6

THE NIGER MISSION
and RACIAL TENSION

(1875–1891)[1]

THE SUSTAINED REPLANTING OF CHRISTIANITY in Nigeria in 1842, which went beyond the coastlines to the interior, was like light penetrating darkness, bringing the transformation of the gospel to spiritually unenlightened worldviews.[2] The CMS was the most visible player in this venture, and the acronym CMS still evokes nostalgia among many native communities in Nigeria as the midwife of Christianity, with its associated benefits of Western education and health facilities, among others. The earliest generations of elite and nationalists—both Christian converts and those who stuck to their religious beliefs—have traced their formation to these initiatives by the CMS. The CMS therefore enjoys the undisputed reputation of a benefactor-institution.

Furthermore, the "recaptives" (liberated African slaves) saw the rehabilitation efforts by the CMS after the abolition of the slave

1. First published in *Anvil* in 2020 as "Racial Tension in Mission: Reviewing the Niger Mission Crisis (1875–97) and Its Implications for Mission." Slightly modified here.

2. This relates to the general human depravity without the light of the gospel, rather than a wholesale condemnation of the African culture as savage.

trade as the restoration of their humanity from the shackles and dehumanization of slavery. It was also a relief to the consciences of their former enslavers.

Invariably, however, history always places events in the dock, and the sweet and the sour, the sentimental and the unsavory, constrain a rethink. The Niger Mission crisis is no exception. That dark period in the otherwise laudable CMS Niger mission encounter has been described as "The Turning of the Tide"[3] by Ade-Ajayi, who saw that period in the 1880s as "a transitional period, a decade of conflict and bitter racial feeling, of schismatic movements in all the existing missions, except of course, the Catholic."[4] Olaseinde Ajayi refers to the period 1873–1885 as "The End of an Era, (The Gathering Storm),"[5] highlighting the early administrative issues that insinuated that the African mission agents were unfit for any meaningful work in the mission. Sanneh refers to it as "The Debacle . . . years of turmoil," highlighting how, by some unusual appointments, Hutchinson as Lay Secretary of the CMS undermined the legitimate roles of Bishop Crowther and virtually scandalized the enormous goodwill the Mission enjoyed.[6] Jesse Page writes about "storm clouds" and "The Crucible" but considered it needless to recount issues that had passed with time.[7] F. K. Elechi calls it "The End of An Era."[8]

The Hopeful Years and the First Signs of Racial Tension

Two key players come into focus in the administrative contrasts that played out, favorably at first, and tragically at a later stage. They are the CMS Secretaries Henry Venn (from 1841–1877) and his successor, Edward Hutchinson (Lay Secretary from 1872–82).

3. Ade-Ajayi, *Christian Missions in Nigeria*, 233.

4. Ade-Ajayi, *Christian Missions*, 235.

5. Ajayi, "History of the Niger and Northern Nigeria Missions," 191.

6. Sanneh, "CMS and the African Transformation," 192.

7. Page, *Black Bishop*, 199.

8. Ekechi, *Missionary Enterprise and Rivalry*, 57.

Both played critical roles in the events that shaped history in different directions.[9]

Henry Venn's "three-selfs" principle of a native church that would be self-propagating, self-financing, and self-governing advocated that the foreign missionary moves on to the regions beyond which would allow "the euthanasia of a mission."[10]

Ajayi Crowther, the rescued slave boy, became the principal actor in this hopeful venture. He kept close to his heart the unrepayable debt of gratitude he owed to the CMS. He was rescued on 7th April 1822 by the English patrol (men-of-war) and nurtured by the CMS in Sierra Leone. Whatever he became thereafter, he owed to the kind-heartedness of the CMS. They taught him the gospel, baptized him (on 11th Dec 1925), trained him, put him on the second Niger Expedition in 1841, and influenced his ordination in 1843 and his subsequent consecration as bishop in 1864. Henry Venn, the CMS General Secretary, might well be called the chief architect of much of these developments. There was much goodwill and commitment from the supporting churches in England as reports from the mission field acquainted them with the progress and needs of the Mission. His charge at his first Synod in 1866 captures much of this:

> Eleven long and hopeless years rolled away before another effort was made. The heart of the late Mr. McGregor Laird was stirred up. This benevolent English merchant, whom nothing daunted, determined to make another effort, and being backed by Her Majesty's government, in 1854 he planned out an exploring expedition to the Tshadda branch ('sic') of the Niger, which proved successful beyond all expectations. Being thus encouraged in 1857 the visit was repeated, with attempts to establish trading stations at given points, where also a Christian Mission was to be commenced among the people. From this period we date the commencement of this Mission. The period from 1842 to 1854 had been indeed a time of severe trial to the faith of God's praying people. He at last

9. Stock, "History of the CMS," 3:39.
10. Shenk, *Henry Venn*, 118–25.

answered their prayers, when, in 1857, a beginning was made of a Christian Mission on the banks of the Niger.

He continues with more specific locations, "Our first station was commenced at Onitsha in 1857 . . . the next place attempted to be secured for a Mission-station was Gbebe, at the confluence of the Kwara and Tshadda rivers . . . " He further states that the pioneer workers located there were "three readers, Messrs James Thomas, Edward Klein, and Jacob Newland."[11] Kolapo's dating from the journals of one of these pioneer workers, James Thomas, puts the commencement of the work within the same period: "The Gbebe CMS station opened in September 1858, eight years before the civil war,"[12] but in less than a decade a civil war dispersed both missionaries and converts:

> In 1865, a vicious civil war broke out in Gbebe, dispersing its population, and rendering the town totally unsafe for any meaningful work. This crisis took the better part of a decade to resolve itself. Meanwhile the mission agents relocated to Lokoja where a mission station had begun the previous year. Hence, in Lokoja, apart from the Trinity Church and mission house over which Rev. Thomas. C. John presided, there existed also the Bunu/Oworo chapel that was in the total charge of James Thomas.[13]

As the possibility of Crowther becoming a bishop crystalized, Henry Townsend, also a pioneer CMS missionary, based in Abeokuta, mobilized every possible effort to resist this on racial grounds, until it became unconcealed rivalry and hostility. His correspondence with the home office was dominated with arguments emphasizing white supremacy over the black man, sometimes using inflammatory language, sometimes even contradicting himself. According to him, "Native teachers of whatever grade have

---

11. Crowther, *Charge Delivered on the Banks,* 8.

12. Kolapo, "Extra-Religious Encounters," 90.

13. Crowther, *Charge Delivered on the Banks,* 18.

been received and respected by the chiefs and people only as being the agents or servants of white men."[14]

Townsend was so strong in his distrust of black leadership that he opposed the ordination of even people like T. B. Macaulay, who had been trained at the same CMS training institution at Islington where he himself had been trained. The same objection was extended to Theophilus King, who had been a capable catechist at Lokoja in 1841, and had trained at Fourah Bay, becoming Crowther's able assistant in translation. As he put it, "I have great doubt of young black clergymen. They want years of experience to give stability to their characters; we would rather have them as schoolmasters and catechists."[15] His views were shared by most of the white missionaries, and at one point even the Home Office felt constrained to caution about the tone of his letter which had become unworthy of his vocation.[16]

Evaluating the progress of the mission at the approach of its 65th anniversary, an article in the *Church Missionary Intelligencer* asked probing questions and provided hopeful answers. This evaluation saw much potential in the possibility of the African Christian being entrusted with the task ahead:

> Already the African Christian has been tried in this service. He has shown himself not only capable of understanding and receiving the truth of Christianity, but of communicating it to his fellow-countrymen. On him the African climate exercises no malign influence; to him the languages of Africa present no impediment. [17]

The writer became more specific in pointing to Ajayi Crowther:

> The native evangelist has been tried and found to be reliable. We, at first, doubted him and feared to use him; but providential circumstances compelled us to bring him forward. . . . He has been tried alone on the banks of the

14. Ade-Ajayi, *Christian Missions*, 181.

15. Ade-Ajayi, *Christian Missions*, 181.

16. Sanneh, "CMS and the African Transformation," 190.

17. *Church Missionary Intelligencer* (March 1890), "Thoughts in Relation to The Approaching Anniversary," 97.

Niger. No white brother stood by him there to counsel and direct him. . . . Withdrawn from European superintendence, he has realized the presence of God, and walked conscientiously and in the fear of the Lord.[18]

He asks where such an African clergyman could be found to be entrusted with the episcopal responsibility, and pointed to the positive testimony of the CMS about the Rev. Samuel Crowther, who by then had put in nearly twenty-one fruitful years of ordained ministry: "To delay any longer the native Episcopate would be unduly to retard the development of the native church."[19]

His biographer, Jesse Page, remarks that on the day of his consecration, 29th June 1864, it had been arranged that Crowther should be presented by the two colonial bishops present, but in the palpable excitement of the event, "the Bishop of Winchester, with kindly thoughtfulness, stepped forward, and waving aside Bishop Nixon, took his place beside Crowther, so on such an occasion a double honor should be rendered to the African prelate," walking him up to the Archbishop.[20]

Bishop Crowther's Ambiguous Episcopal Jurisdiction

Even though Henry Venn jubilantly called it the "full development of the native African Church,"[21] his enthusiasm was not shared by the other white missionaries on the field. His jurisdiction was ambiguously delineated as "the countries of Western Africa beyond the limits of our dominions."[22] Unpacking that vague description, Ade-Ajayi traced it as "West Africa from the Equator to the

---

18. *Church Missionary Intelligencer* (March 1890), "Thoughts in Relation to The Approaching Anniversary," 97.

19. *Church Missionary Intelligencer* (March 1890), "Thoughts in Relation to The Approaching Anniversary," 97.

20. Page, *Black Bishop,* 188.

21. Ade-Ajayi, *Christian Missions in Nigeria,* 208.

22. Ade-Ajayi, *Christian Missions in Nigeria,* 206.

Senegal, with the exception of the British colonies of Lagos, the Gold Coast and Sierra Leone."[23]

In a diocese so vast, with a mandate so ambiguous, Crowther was based in Lagos for administrative convenience, and yet Lagos was not part of his diocese, for the whites were there; and it was not considered a good idea that white men should be seen to be under the authority of a black man.[24] His work spread to Igboland but administrative problems and other difficulties like transportation and the lack of cooperation of the British traders of the Royal Niger Company and white colleagues, such as Townsend and the others in the Yoruba Mission, made his ministry turbulent, especially towards the end. Venn had written, appealing to each of the European missionaries, "Be you a brother to Bishop Crowther. You will be abundantly repaid. God destines him for a great work. I should rejoice to be a helper, however, to him."[25] Townsend would have none of that, nor would any of the European missionaries. It was a shocking realization for the Parent Committee.

Crowther faced other challenges, for most of the workers he recruited came from Sierra Leone and were more interested in comfortable conditions and their status than the sacrifices that the ministry demanded. Some of his assistants had serious moral lapses. In Bonny, for instance, a pioneer agent, J. K. Webber raped a ten-year-old schoolgirl, and there were similar cases about that same time. All these reflected badly on Crowther's administrative competence.

Ade-Ajayi further identified the key figure of this period to be James Johnson—otherwise called "Holy Johnson"—who was not prepared to play along with the hypocritical contradictions of the European missionaries who felt the African was to be marginalized and treated as an underdog, whatever his ability. Ajayi felt "he was a reformer, not a revolutionary."[26] African mission agents and traders were lumped together and treated alike, with

23. Ade-Ajayi, *Christian Missions in Nigeria,* 206.

24. Décorvet and Oladipo, *Samuel Ajayi Crowther,* 102.

25. Ade-Ajayi, *Christian Missions,* 195.

26. Ade-Ajayi, *Christian Missions,* 236..

scandalous reports made about them. Because European commercial interests were at stake, these negative reports continued to be sent to the CMS Home Office at Salisbury Square, which of course Bishop Crowther stoutly and consistently defended. He felt rather that the European traders didn't take kindly to the question of Sunday observance and substantiated his report with a quotation traced to one Cliff, who was the local agent of Holland, Jacques & Co., that "the institution of Sunday was an invention of rascally, mischievous black missionaries unknown to the white man."[27] Ajayi observed that "The persistent reports of the Europeans were gradually undermining the confidence the CMS previously had in African missionaries."[28]

Deteriorating Missionary Spirituality

Henry Johnson and James Johnson were friends, not brothers. But they were both highly educated and shared a passion for forthrightness in the face of declining relational ethics in the missionary group for reasons of racial prejudice. For instance, they were both more vocal than Bishop Crowther, and clearly less accommodating of the pretensions of a good number of the European missionaries, especially where they communicated racial tendencies in what was to be a fellowship of brothers. While Henry Johnson saw no need to condone the moral lapses of some native agents, he was of the view that reform was welcome, but went further to observe that it was "the unconcealed contempt with which we are being treated that tries me so much."[29]

Bishop Crowther's Humiliation

Things began to unfold very quickly as one thing led inevitably to another. The distrust in Crowther's ability to run a "purely native

27. Ade-Ajayi, *Christian Missions*, 240.

28. Ade-Ajayi, *Christian Missions*, 240.

29. Ekechi, *Missionary Enterprise and Rivalry*, 61.

mission"[30] became more pronounced. When his mission support-
ers in England provided a steamer named after Henry Venn for his
missionary work, he placed it in the hands of an African merchant
with the intention of making it pay its way by trading on the Niger
and to provide for the mission from its profits. The European merchants insinuated that it would be used in competition with their
business interest rather than propagating the gospel. Hutchinson,
the sitting CMS Lay Secretary, overruled Crowther by appointing
J. H. Ashcroft, a European lay agent, to take over the financial and
administrative responsibilities of the Niger Mission in 1879. According to him, it was to relieve Bishop Crowther of the concerns
about the temporal affairs of the mission and leave his "mind free
for the more solemn and important spiritual duties,"[31] It turned
out to be actually a demotion of the bishop, for the steamer was
hardly available to him even for his episcopal visits.

Though Bishop Crowther was willing to welcome Ashcroft,
the administrative anomalies of this arrangement became evident,
for the latter saw this position as one that placed him in supervision
over Bishop Ajayi Crowther. When the brewing power struggle
surfaced and escalated into a full-blown crisis, Hutchinson and the
CMS had more confidence in the account of the European laymen
than in Bishop Ajayi Crowther, who was their own man. The racial
and commercial discrimination could no longer be concealed. By
1880, a Commission of Inquiry was set up to look into the affairs
of the mission.

Rev. J. B. Wood, the Secretary of the Commission, wrote a
damaging report which charged African mission agents with serious offenses and scandalous crimes ranging from immorality to
manslaughter. Not only was it published in England, the content
was made available to European merchants of the Royal Niger
Company, but not to the bishop. The lack of consensus in opinion
at the home office concerning these damaging allegations, with
no input from the Bishop himself, necessitated the setting up of
a committee consisting of Hutchinson and Rev. J. B. Whitting to

---

30. Ade-Ajayi, *Christian Missions*, 195.

31. Tasie, *Christian Missionary Enterprise*, 89.

investigate the situation more objectively. Rev. Whitting was more sympathetic to the African perspective and the need for a fair hearing. The meeting was held at Madeira in March 1881, but Rev. Wood, who wrote the report, was absent. Bishop Ajayi Crowther, however, had his opportunity to defend the allegations by placing the accusations in their proper context. He was fully exonerated. Far-reaching decisions were taken to redress the situation: a training institution was recommended for Lokoja, a pay raise was approved to encourage the African agents' wives to give up trading and be fully devoted to the ministry with their husbands. Hutchinson, Ashcroft, and Kirk, who were the key collaborators, either resigned or were dismissed. Within this turbulent period, Bishop Crowther suffered the loss of his mother and the prolonged ill health and eventual death of his dear wife.

Bishop Crowther's Limitation as a Disciplinarian

It must be conceded that the charge of administrative incompetence brought against Bishop Ajayi Crowther had to do with the discipline of his workers. In Ade-Ajayi's view, however, Bishop Ajayi Crowther was a pastor at heart and was not inclined to dismissing erring staff even when they deserved it. Rather, he preferred the soft and hopeful option of suspension as an opportunity for reflection, repentance, and restoration. He was more concerned about reclaiming the prodigal rather than losing them. Ade-Ajayi, however, concedes that "for a pioneer he was too reasonable, too soft a disciplinarian." That notwithstanding, the insolence of the young missionaries who came to discredit Bishop Ajayi Crowther's longstanding achievements was inexcusable. He described them as "able, young, zealous, impetuous, uncharitable and opinionated." The oldest of them, the Rev. J. A. Johnson, was only twenty-nine.[32]

---

32. Ade-Ajayi, *Christian Missions*, 250.

Ethiopianism

The missionary enterprise, which had been struggling to extricate itself from the stranglehold of colonial complicity, found itself on a collision course with the eruption of nationalistic passions in the form of Ethiopianism—an African nationalist movement expressed through the medium of the church and inspired by Psalm 68:31. The notion that "Ethiopia shall stretch forth her hands to God" was fast gaining ground in the period from 1875 to 1890. According to Ayandele, its legitimacy was on solid ground:

> Unrestricted access to the Bible, with its notions of equality, justice and non-racialism, provided the early converts with a valid weapon which they were not reluctant to employ against the missionaries who brushed these ideas aside in Church administration and in their relations with the converts.[33]

A major feature was the assertion of racial independence in both politics and mission. Prominent Africans like James Johnson (Holy Johnson) and Mojola Agbebi, who were highly educated, were front-liners even as key mission staff, the one CMS, the other Baptist.

There were other far-reaching effects of the humiliation of Crowther. The Nigerian Baptists, seeing what had happened, and with their Southern Baptist missionaries withdrawn during the American Civil War, asserted their control of the mission, and by 1888 broke away as the Native Baptist Church, taking with them the great African pioneers. Agbebi was the key player.

At Lokoja, where the CMS had its key mission station in the Upper Niger Mission, the same factors of racism and high-handedness were played out, and Ayandele confirms the impressions about Christianity in Lokoja at this time from the perspective of the young breed of missionaries. This was "The Sudan Team," formed in the University of Cambridge by ardent youngsters imbued with the spirit of revival sweeping the country at the time. The teachings of Moody and Sankey encouraged them to mission

---

33. Ayandele, *Missionary Impact,* 176.

and the establishment of a church devoid of frivolities and sin. Crowther was delighted to receive such ardent young helpers when the CMS decided to send them to Lokoja.[34] However, the approach of the new arrivals was uncompromising in the extreme. They branded all the converts in Lokoja adulterers and harlots and dismissed them from church membership until they confessed their iniquities one by one; the Muslims were told that the African missionaries who had been working in Lokoja were not Christians but *kafiris,* that is, infidels.[35]

Graham William Brooke, the leader of the team in Lokoja, was unambiguously uncharitable, for he felt the whole structure that had existed had to be pulled down before they could start afresh:

> We are driven to admit that there is no hope of success until we have first taken down the whole of the past work so that no one stone remains upon another. I mean that the pastors . . . must be changed, the communicants must be changed, the message preached must be changed, the time, mode and place of worship must be changed, the school children must be changed and the course in the schools must be changed.[36]

That was not all. For the Finance Committee meeting of August 1890, members of the Sudan Team came with a list of names of priests they had suspended from ministry for the bishop to ratify. When the bishop explained that they had no ecclesiastical authority over other staff, some of whom had been priests for longer than they had been alive, they insisted that they were exercising authority vested in them by the CMS, and they proceeded to launch vile insults on the bishop himself.[37]

With the dismissal of many African agents, new appointments and restructuring arbitrarily carried out without sensitivity to the African personnel, the person and position of the venerable

---

34. Décorvet and Oladipo, *Samuel Ajayi Crowther,* 151–53.

35. Ayandele, *Missionary Impact,* 215.

36. Ekechi, *Missionary Enterprise and Rivalry,* 65.

37. Décorvet and Oladipo, *Samuel Ajayi Crowther,* 164.

old bishop rudely assaulted, he felt constrained to dictate his resignation. Ade-Ajayi makes this sobering and haunting comment on the scenario: "Few scenes could have been more painful to watch than the grey-haired old Bishop of over 80 active years, tormented and insulted by the young Europeans, trembling with rage as he never trembled before, as he got up to announce his resignation from the committee."[38]

Décorvet and Oladipo further observed:

> The news soon spread, and nationalist sentiments rose to a level never seen before. The Africans, be they Christians, pagans or Muslims, were outraged. Protests poured in. The Emir of Bida decided to expel all English missionaries from his emirate. It was not only the bishop that had been insulted but the entire black race through the person of their most eminent representative.[39]

There followed various ploys by the Parent Committee to uproot the octogenarian bishop and carry out certain radical reforms without regard to the loss of face for him. The mission was split into two: the upper half of the Niger Mission was under the twenrty-five-year-old Graham William Brooke, leader of the Sudan Party, based in Lokoja; and the lower Niger, with headquarters at Onitsha, would remain under Bishop Crowther, but be controlled by a finance committee under the leadership of members of the Sudan Party. According to Ajayi, it is in the context of these instances of scheming, that the gold of Bishop Crowther's character shines forth, as we see in his response below, which is without bitterness:

> If others are delicate to tell me of my incompetence in the superintendence of the Niger Mission, it is my duty to relieve their minds of that delicacy. I am ready to yield place to others to act as leading managers of the Niger Mission. I am willing, as long as my health lasts, to labor as a pioneer in opening fresh grounds, while the already

38. Ade-Ajayi. *Christian Missions*, 253.

39. Décorvet and Oladipo, *Samuel Ajayi Crowther*, 165.

established stations can be worked by superior intellects and better managers.[40]

This certainly was the picture of a house divided against itself and was by no means a positive image of the mission. Tasie's work, *Christian Missionary Enterprise in the Niger Delta* 1864–1918, takes a penetrating missiological look at the factors that have often been sentimentalized by social and political historians. For him, these nationalistic interpretations undermined the critical importance of a strong ethical foundation that was required in the encounter of Christianity with the indigenous worldview that they sought to influence at this time. He pitched the issues against the fundamental ethics and teaching of Christianity. Beginning from the leadership question, he observes that even though Bishop Ajayi Crowther was physically, mentally, psychologically, and spiritually equipped for the difficult ministry terrain of the Niger Delta mission, he was clearly weak as an administrator and disciplinarian.

The Aftermath of the Niger Mission Crisis

K. O. Dike provides a sympathetic assessment of this tumultuous time that has been prone to many frenzied interpretations:

> Throughout the last ten years of his episcopate, Crowther was painfully aware of the evils that assailed the Mission from within. It may be that as a leader he was too gentle, too soft for a pioneer, relying as he did on guiding his staff by persuasion and example rather than by strict disciplinary measures. But as already indicated he was working against heavy odds, and it is against the background of his immense difficulties that he must ultimately be judged. Looking back the historian is impressed not by the Bishop's failures but by his successes: had Crowther been given the tools required for the job, most of the short-comings of his Mission could have been avoided.[41]

---

40. Quoted in Epelle, *Promise of Nigeria*, 36.
41. Dike, *Origins of the Niger Mission,* 20.

Three strands appeared to have emerged from the crisis. The CMS remained rigid about having nothing short of flawless native agents, while the native agents would not entertain any consideration about CMS actions being anything other than racial prejudice. Neither the CMS nor the African agents seemed to have taken into serious account the shift from the earlier days of Buxton and Venn, who had faith in the contribution of the African to the missionary enterprise in Africa. While the new missionaries were obsessed with the urgency of evangelization, the African elite were becoming increasingly nationalistic in their disposition especially in the face of mass displacement of native agents.

Tasie concludes with the opinion that the African agents "were not dismissed because they were Africans but because their standards did not measure up to the responsibility they bore for the spiritual welfare of their congregations."[42]

The matter of a successor to Bishop Crowther only protracted the crises, as it went to Joseph Sidney Hill who had earlier been a CMS missionary in West Africa. To assuage the bruised feelings and dashed expectations, two African clergy, namely Charles Philips and Isaac Oluwole, were made assistant bishops. That an African bishop was not appointed to replace Crowther confirmed the suspicion that the view of some missionaries about the racial supremacy of the Europeans was upheld. The fallout was played out in many places and in many ways, the most significant being the rapid spread of the African church and the independent African churches. European missionaries became the main personnel of the CMS in the Lokoja area for a long time, even though they did not all exhibit racist tendencies. Indeed, some of them blended so well with the indigenous culture in many parts of the North, such as the Nupe and Hausa missions. In later years, McIntyre, Claud Daintree, Dr. Walter Miller, and Max Warren, among several others became part of the communities. However, this scenario of white domination of the missionary scene in both CMS and sister mission organizations like SUM and SIM made the mission

---

42 Tasie, *Christian Missionary Enterprise,* 134.

churches essentially foreign in outlook and delayed the process of indigenization.

One of the most succinct descriptions of Bishop Crowther's life is given by Eugene Stock in his preface to the biography by Jesse Page: "He lived in an atmosphere of suspicion and scandal, yet no tongue, however malicious, ventured to whisper reproach against his personal character. Some might criticize his administration; no one ever questioned his sincerity and simplicity."[43]

Lamin Sanneh's summary of the entire episode is quite sobering, if not indeed haunting:

> The momentous drama in which Bishop Crowther was intended as the sacrificial victim had been confidently staged on the dismantled policy of Henry Venn, with missionary lightweights propped up to challenge Crowther's Episcopal authority and alienate his achievement. Through irregular procedural arrangements, the CMS allowed Crowther to be outflanked until the substantive powers he held as bishop were effectively curtailed, his priestly stature was diminished and the man himself was reduced to a sorry sight.[44]

Not every European missionary felt the same way as their racist colleagues. Archdeacon Henry Dobinson, Secretary of the Niger Mission, was to write later,

> I greatly long to see an African Diocese formed. I would like to see Lagos and Bonny united under, say, James Johnson in a coast Diocese . . . I do rejoice that Archn Hy Johnson is again established. I burn with shame and horror now at the awful charges made against him in 1890 . . . May God forgive us the bitter slanderous and lying thoughts we had against him and others in those dark days of 1890 . . . We have suffered, no one knows how much, by those rash and hasty actions. We condemned others and we ourselves have done less than they did . . . .

---

43. Page, *Black Bishop,* vii.

44. Sanneh, *West African Christianity,* 169.

I now repudiate the slanders and accusations brought against Johnson and Crowther.[45]

Dr. C. F. Hartford-Battersby, who had served at the medical missions, was another. But the high-handed Brooke edged him out. Even though the Parent Committee was said to be disappointed by Dobinson's submissions, he stood his ground.

Many reparatory steps have been taken since then, resulting in the recognition and reabsorption of the Niger Delta Pastorate that had disconnected in the wake of the crises. There has been expansion of CMS work in other areas, such as the medical work at Iyi Enu from the 1890s, Teacher Training College at Awka, then to Egbu, Patani, and Isoko by 1910. In Western Nigeria, the CMS Bookshop was opened in Lagos. In Northern Nigeria, work among the Nupe, where Crowther had interacted considerably in earlier years, began in earnest by 1903. The hospital at Ado Ekiti followed in 1936, while expansion into Hausa land in 1905 by Dr. Walter Miller all became the brighter side of the mission story.

The commendable efforts at resolving the crisis notwithstanding, the sad implications still showed up in the Diocese of Lagos. On the eve of Nigerian independence (1st October 1960) the parish where the Governor General worshipped, then known as St. Savior's Church, amended their constitution to ensure they were not under the Episcopal oversight of a black bishop. By the inauguration of the Church of Nigeria as an autonomous Province on 24th February 1979, they were still hiring and firing their clergy without reference to the bishop. This face-off continued until matters were resolved by the Nigerian military government, which decreed that all Anglican churches come under the authority of the Nigerian bishop enthroned. The decree was gazetted (as Decree 26, 1991). Archbishop Joseph Adelitoye changed the name of the parish to Our Savior's Church as a part of the Diocese of Lagos.[46]

Several decades after, these issues were never far from the mind of the African Christian, especially Anglicans. A clear

---

45. Dobinson, "Letter to Baylis," G3A3/1896/54.
46. Our Saviour's Church, TBS, Lagos, *From Colonial to Cosmopolitan*, 195.

indication is the theme that was considered at the First African Anglican Conference in 2004: *Africa Comes of Age*. The suspicion of unchanging imperialist tendencies remains an ever-present challenge, as ample reasons have persisted down through subsequent generations.

At the 150th anniversary of the consecration of Bishop Crowther in 2014, the 105th Archbishop of Canterbury, Justin Welby, held a service of thanksgiving on 29th June, with representatives of the Church of Nigeria (Anglican Communion) in attendance. In his sermon, Welby said:

> This is a service of thanksgiving and repentance. Thanksgiving for the extraordinary life, which we commemorate, and repentance, shame and sorrow for Anglicans who are reminded of the sin of many of their ancestors. . . . We in the Church of England need to say sorry that someone was properly and rightly consecrated Bishop and then betrayed and let down and undermined. It was wrong. . . . In spite of immense hardship and despite the racism of many whites, he evangelized so effectively that he was eventually ordained Bishop, over much protest. He led his missionary diocese brilliantly but was in the end falsely accused and had to resign, not long before his death.

The archbishop then warned the congregation not to condemn Crowther's opponents without holding up a mirror to today's church: "Whom do we exclude by reason of race . . . or in our desire for power?"[47]

47. Davies, "Canterbury Remembers Crowther," para. 5.

Chapter 7

RESPONSE *to the* MISSIONARY ENCOUNTER

THE LOKOJA NIGER-BENUE CONFLUENCE AREA has, through decades of crosscultural encounter, become the epitome of harmonious coexistence and a flagship of the highly valued ideal of religious tolerance. While the area attracted people from different social classes who were brought together by such exigencies as commercial pursuits, slavery, colonial administration, and religious devotion, the missionary heritage has become the strongest bond for a harmonious coexistence with value-driven social institutions that endure. This has manifested in the integration fostered by the educational, health, and social institutions put in place by CMS, and indeed in later years also by others such as the Roman Catholic Mission and the Qua Iboe Mission.

The multinationals that had dominated the commercial scene (e.g., J. Fairley and Co., Pagenstecker and Co., H. Siegler and Co., John Holt, and the United Africa Company) gradually plummeted in their significance within the immediate environment. This was a factor of changing political fortunes, such as the relocation of the seat of colonial administration first from Lokoja to Zungeru and then to Kaduna, and the transfer of Marine Headquarters to Forcados in 1914. Yet CMS consolidated its impact as a grassroots movement, influencing converts, traditional institutions, and indeed the Muslim community.

At every point of analyzing the response of the Niger-Benue Confluence to the missionary presence, and its aftermath, the pre-Christian setting must always be borne in mind. The postabolition economic crises in the coastal states of the Yoruba, Igbo, and Brass communities precipitated the search for a viable alternative as provided by the allurements that came with missionary Christianity in the form of commercial and military aid, as well as education. But the communities around the Lokoja Niger-Benue Confluence remained firmly in the grip of the Nupe emirate, with the strong factor of military aid from the jihadists. Indeed, missionary advance had to be negotiated on the premise of military advantage accruing from the colonial government to the reigning Nupe monarch, Etsu Massaba. Under such circumstances, slave trafficking in such interiors thrived unchecked, and effective missionary incursion was greatly restrained by the entrenched Islamic militancy, leaving only those at the fringes of society—rather than the elite—to embrace the new faith.

At the early stages, before the zealous, young, evangelistic Cambridge missionaries (The Sudan Party) came on the scene, Bishop Ajayi Crowther had adopted a more sensitive, diplomatic, and strategic approach to the prejudices of the Muslim communities among whom he worked. According to Kolapo, Crowther "hoped to impart modernization via educational or technical and commercial knowledge as the practical side of the theological and ritual aspect of the missionaries' enterprise."[1]

Until the arrival of colonial administrators, this method of education continued side by side with the indigenous pattern of socialization that the missionaries met on the ground (viz., oral transmission of cultural values, and the performance of rites and rituals). The full context that now emerged was that, alongside missionary education, the religious education provided by Muslims through their Quranic schools served as a counterpart. For the education provided at that level, the Islamic holy book, the

1. Kolapo, *Christian Missionary Engagement*, 248.

Qu'ran, was the basic text for the converts. There were, of course, higher levels to which outstanding pupils could attain and there is no reason to suppose that the practice in the Lokoja Niger-Benue Confluence area was an exception to the general practice of pre-colonial Islamic education as Andrew E. Barnes notes:

> Teachers would gather children in a semi-circle in front of them and write out a passage from the Koran with chalk on a piece of slate. The teacher would explain the meaning of the passage while the students memorized it. *Kuttab* schools fed into *medrasah*, schools of higher learning taught by masters who represented various Islamic brotherhoods. Only students who displayed some real command of the sacred writings would make it to this stage. At these higher schools they would acquire a systematic understanding of various interpretations of the Koran, an introduction to other forms of Islamic literature and training in logic and mathematics.[2]

That there has been considerable vitriol over allegations of cultural imperialism spearheaded by missionaries is no longer news in scholarly circles. Besides, some critics have failed to separate European missionaries from European colonialists. For this reason, misdemeanors from either side have been smeared on both parties rather indiscriminantly. Cases abound to lend credence to the insinuations of compromise in attitudes, but so do instances abound to justify the opinion that the primary intentions of the missionaries and colonialists were not one and the same. Andrew Porter summarizes the general impression about the missionaries by critics:

> Missions were the van of Europe's expansion. Once their bridgeheads were established, the presence and teaching of missionaries ridiculed indigenous beliefs, called customs into question, undermined self-confidence, eroded respect for traditional authorities, and consequently stimulated political or social conflict. Thus debilitated, indigenous societies gave way to the broader pressures of

2. Barnes, *Making Headway,* 142.

western expansion; internal collapse and irresistible cultural change opened the way to direct colonial rule. This was paralleled by the imposition of missionary categories of thought and belief, and associated with continuing missionary control of education and the churches. Missionaries were thus prime agents of an intrusive 'cultural imperialism.'[3]

Bishop Crowther as the Midwife of Traditional Rulership in Lokoja

The foundation of tolerance laid by the pioneer missionaries consolidated the practice of communal religious posture in the communities, for religious observances and cultural practices were inseparable in most cases. It is well documneted that Ajayi Crowther was an untiring crusader of religious tolerance in teaching and practice, as is well documented in a number of records, but notably by Peter McKenzie. Andrew Walls also cites the significant perspective modeled by Ajayi Crowther:

> Crowther's early experience in Sierra Leone had taught him that confrontation where one party cries "Jesus is the Son of God" and the other "No, he is not" was useless. In his mature years on the Niger, he sought for common ground at the nexus of Qur'an and Bible: the themes of the status of Jesus as a great prophet, his miraculous birth, Gabriel as the messenger of God[4]

When Islam came on the scene as the first of the two foreign religions introduced to the communities of the Niger-Benue Confluence, it brought with it the authority of the emirate, thus claiming the allegiance of the traditional rulers. This was a convenient arrangement to ensure military protection and loyalty from the British traders and colonialists. In Lokoja itself for instance, the position of the Maigari was first occupied by a convert of the CMS,

3. Porter, "'Cultural Imperialism,'" 367.
4. Walls, *Cross-Cultural Process*, 144.

Jacob Mieux, who was recommended by Bishop Ajayi Crowther, and in this capacity was the one entrusted with the ambassadorial task of being the intermediary between the British government and the Nupe emirate. This became necessary by this time because the consulate at Lokoja had become quite expensive to maintain. Indeed, when the British government declined appointing a consul to Lokoja following the withdrawal of British personnel by the West African Company in 1872–1873, Crowther became the *de facto* consul, appropriately described by Ade-Ajayi as "an undesignated consul on the river."[5] In this role he conveyed presents and correspondence from the British government to the Emir of Bida, Etsu Massaba, and in turn took his own presents that were to be sent to the queen. Crampton notes that "Crowther always treated the Etsu with great respect believing that it was better to deal with a ruler who kept order, even though he was a pagan or a Muslim, rather than a people in a state of anarchy."[6] It was in this context that Jacob Mieux was recommended by Crowther and Lieutenant Molyneux to the Emir of Bida, Etsu Massaba, as the official representative at Lokoja. As the arrangement was concluded, it was ratified by the signature of the emir and the bishop:

> A decree of 12 September 1870, bearing signature in Arabic of Emir Massaba and signed by S.A. Crowther, Bishop, Niger Territory, as witness, made known to the agents of the mercantile factories, the missionary station, all English subjects, settlers and natives, residing at Lokoja, the Emir's expressed wish that the settlement of Lokoja should be well populated as a chief mart at the Confluence.[7]

As the flag-bearer of Usman Dan Fodio, who wielded extensive powers over much of the North, the Etsu Massaba required all those to be appointed into traditional leadership under his domain to be converted to Islam. C. A. M. Lakpini also alluded to this

---

5. Ade-Ajayi, *Christian Missions*, 214.

6. Crampton, *Christianity in Northern Nigeria*, 21.

7. Pedraza, *Borrioboola-Gha*, 71.

when he traced the advent of Islam to Bassa Nge country, a part of the communities in the Niger-Benue Confluence area:

> Mayaki Etan, the Etsu, on reaching Bida, was initiated into Islamic religion by persuasion of the Emir of Bida. This was exactly what happened to the then reigning Maigari of Lokoja who was a Christian and was attending the Holy Trinity Anglican Church, Lokoja, before he was taken to Bida for recognition by the Emir. As a matter of fact, the first two reigning Maigaris of Lokoja, namely, HRH Jacob Mieux popularly known as Musa Maigari (1870) and HRH Daniel Abiga (1902) were Christians before they were converted to Islam.[8]

However, in terms of leadership in the Muslim community, the situation was different concerning the position of the chief Imam in Lokoja, which was dominated by the Nupe in what was considered by some as an overt display of diabolical powers among contestants. On this, Suleiman notes below,

> There is no available explanation as to how they established such a dominant position in the leadership of the central mosque. It is, however, not unlikely that the issue dates back to the time when the first chief of Lokoja–Musa Maigari (1870–1896) was appointed. Since he was a Hausa, it is possible that a Nupe man was appointed to the chair of the Imamship in order to create a balance between the two largest ethnic groups. In any case, one thing is clear, no Hausa scholar ever sought for the leadership of the central mosque . . . no reasonable Hausa person would have accepted such a position even if given when the Nupe were fighting each other with charm in order to get such a position, and the relationship between the Nupe and the Hausa was not cordial.[9]

In all these, it is noteworthy that the traditional ruling council of Lokoja has maintained this cordiality with the Christians, mostly the Anglican Church, which was established here by the

---

8. Lakpini, *History of Bassa (Nge)*, 94–95.

9. Suleiman, *Hausa in Lokoja*, 66.

CMS, who were the missionaries on the ground and the proprietors of the mission schools under reference in this study.

Alhaji Mohammadu Kabir Maikarfi III, Maigari of Lokoja, confirms that,

> The first Maigari, Musa, was a Christian, baptized with the name Jacob Mieux. It was at Bida that he was converted to Islam because the Massaba said, as a flag bearer of Usman Dan Fodio he couldn't have a Christian ruler reigning under him. Abiga also was a member of the Anglican Church and was required to convert. The kingship does not rotate. The kingmakers are three: the Chief Imam, a Clergyman, and the ward heads of the different wards. They then recommend someone from any of the three ruling houses who will become the next Maigari (as the Kaduna traditional rulers were also called then). Their criteria is usually to find someone who will not be biased along narrow sentiments. If someone of the stature of Bishop Crowther had to recommend and witness the appointment of the first Maigari, then whoever wants to succeed must work closely with the Christians especially Anglicans. That is why presently we have these traditional titles in Lokoja occupied by Christians: the highly influential position of Galadima in person of Dr. Godwin T.N. Ajakpo; the Marafa in person of Evangelist Emmanuel Yusuf; the Nnayetsu in person of Mrs. Ndalugi (daughter of the Late Canon F.Z. Fearon); the Dalhatu in person of Dr. Edwin Bako; the Lakpini in person of Senator General J.T. Ogbeha (Rtd); the Taga in person of Christopher A.S. H. Bako; and the Kaigama in the person of Hon Peter El Shettima Agbogun.[10]

The Maigari further testifies that a good number of these Christian titleholders were appointed by him to serve on the committee of the newly completed Lokoja Central Mosque and they performed very well.

All major functions in the Anglican Church have had members of the traditional council in attendance. The Maigari attributes the peaceful religious coexistence in Lokoja to the prayers

10. Maigari, in-person Interview on March 27, 2015.

of godly people in the Church and the Mosque. Lokoja Day is celebrated yearly on the weekend closest to September 12, being the day that Jacob Mieux, who became the first Maigari of Lokoja, was enthroned by the Etsu Massaba of Bida. He states further that,

> At school, majority of my friends were all Christians and we still relate very well. We used to have Nativity play in December. You would be surprised how Muslim boys who were taking part were quoting the Bible. Whenever it was time for the play, the whole town–Christians and Muslims would fill the premises. Some would even carry chairs from people's compounds just to have a place to sit.[11]

Crowther's Interfaith Posture

At the time of these developments, Crowther, by this time a bishop, still had great respect for the Muslim leaders and communities even if he did not always agree with their practices. Once, when he started out from Lokoja through Agbaja on the hills overlooking Lokoja, and on to Bida during the Muslim sacred month of Ramadan, he was amazed by the generosity that greeted them all the way even in the domains controlled by the Muslim king and his subjects. McKenzie records: "up to the moment when on December 13th, the firing of eight big guns announced the end of the fast, Crowther's party was not neglected."[12] Crowther himself puts down this record about the generosity of the Muslim king:

> Though the king himself was under the fast as well as his subjects, we were supplied with an abundance of provisions, both cooked and uncooked, to be prepared in our own way; yams, rice, plantains, goats, sheep, poultry of all kinds, turkeys, ducks, fowls, pigeons, milk, oil for lamps and firewood for cooking, besides large bowls of cooked meals every evening. This was plain proof that

---

11. Maigari, in-person Interview on March 27, 2015.
12. McKenzie, *Inter-Religious Encounters,* 57.

the King did not despise us for non-conformity with
their creed.[13]

The Confluence Area as the Trailblazer
in Missions in Northern Nigeria

While it is here conceded that the colonial administration and
the traders also registered their landmarks in other ways such as
agriculture, commerce, the civil service, and the police, the CMS
bestowed on the Lokoja Niger-Benue Confluence area the singular
honor and historical privilege of being the cradle of Christianity
in Northern Nigeria, with many other firsts: the first baptism of
Christian converts in Gbobe in 1862, the first school providing
Western education (the Holy Trinity School, Lokoja in 1865), and
the first confirmation service, among others.

Education as the Bridge-Builder

Benevolent as missionary and Western education appeared, the
enlightenment of the natives for their own sake was never the
primary objective. Rather, education was tailored towards specific predetermined interests. Protestant missionaries in particular
were dependent on the literacy of the converts to enable them to
read the Bible for themselves. For the missionaries, there was no
ambiguity about this, and it was not an altogether new venture
for them, for they simply adapted their traditional role in Europe
where the church had been the trailblazer in the provision of
standard and relevant education. Andrew Barnes points out that,
in fact, European governments borrowed the churches' idea that
"young people learned best when they were provided with stan-
dardized curricula and taught in a building designed for educational purposes."[14]

---

13. Crowther, *Report of the Overland Journey*, 13.

14. Barnes, *Making Headway*, 139.

Bringing in a feminist perspective, Margaret Strobel believes even the female missionaries and reformers "operated ethnocentrically and maternalistically in their attempts at 'improving' the conditions of the indigenous women" and finds their good intentions inexcusable for what she calls "such destructive actions."[15]

Evaluating the logic of these perspectives, Andrew Porter classifies them as the "bland, ultimately unhelpful conclusion that one party's cultural change is almost always another's cultural imperialism."[16] He queries the impression that the reality or coherence of an imperial culture can be assumed, concluding,

> Its existence certainly needs to be established, and scholars should ask whether in fact there existed among missionaries either a sufficient consensus as to their own culture and understanding of Christianity, or an adequate agreement on modes of transmitting it, for the term 'cultural imperialism' to have general explanatory value.[17]

It is an established fact that the Christian missionary influence, especially in the area of education, became a means of liberation and empowerment for the oppressed elements in society such as women and children, besides helping the indigenous communities themselves, to undertake a reconstruction of their past. Elizabeth Isichei's point refutes the feminist claims about the imposition of Western patriarchalism. She found it "much more generally true in Africa that women experience Christianity as empowering. It gave them a place to stand, from which they could bypass or challenge male-dominated sacred worlds."[18]

In the communities across the Niger, such as the Bassa country where Islam had already been introduced, the missionary impact was mostly felt through educational institutions. The first schools were established in Kpata, and then Akabe around

15. Strobel, *European Women,* 51.
16. Porter, "'Cultural Imperialism,'" 371.
17. Porter, "'Cultural Imperialism,'" 372.
18. Isichei, *Varieties of Christian Experience,* 209.

1895. In terms of the congenial religious atmosphere that ensued, we have this record:

> Members of the past and present royal families of the Bassa Nge ruling houses are so interwoven on the point of religion since many are Christians and many are Muslims, that they can find no factors in the two religions to disunite them; if any factors there are, they seem to unite them stronger and more solidly than to divide them. In fact, this is the happy and ideal situation in Bassa Nge land generally, among all and sundry. Christians and Muslims so interact, inter-relate and inter-socialize that one finds it difficult to differentiate between the two religious adherents except at the time of separate religious worship.[19]

It has been an established practice to have Christians and Muslims demonstrate solidarity in the celebration of special festivals of both faiths. When it was Christmas or Easter or even Harvest Thanksgiving, the Muslim neighbors would be under the tree near the church and come into the church to give thank offerings, while the Christians also would be at the site of the *Eid al-Fitr* celebrations to join in the festive procession back to town. This harmonious interrelationship in Lokoja is further attested to by Adamu Baikie in an autobiography that captures his recollections of the Lokoja of yesteryears:

> Lokoja was an entrepot [sic] or a melting pot of some import because people from many parts of the country and beyond converged in Lokoja, which gave the historical town a flavor which transcended ethnic or religious cleavages. There was the heavy presence of "freed slaves," Sierra Leoneans, West Indians, Igbirra Koto, Igbirra Okene, Kakanda, Hausa, Yorubas, Bassa-Nge, Bassa Komo, Igalas, British Missionaries, etc, all blending into the community which gave Lokoja its unique character.[20]

19. Lakpini, *History of Bassa (Nge)*, 96.
20. Baikie, *Against All Odds*, 154–55.

Christianity as a Harmonizing Influence

Nowhere was the missionary legacy better entrenched than in the educational sector. Pupils related freely with one another as they trekked long distances daily to and from their villages to the school locations, as they were taught together in the classrooms, as they played together on the football pitch and other sporting activities, and as they joined hands in different projects such as providing water or sand for the building of new classrooms. In this way they became an indivisible community regardless of religion, tribe, or clan. This was a new expression of the African communal lifestyle in this unique setting. In a report of the Lokoja–Bassa District dated March 15—Nov. 25 1937 by Thomas E. Alvarez, he reports that "The Bishop's Boys Hostel at Akabe is fulfilling its purpose admirably, and some of the boys show considerable promise educationally, as well as in the matter of character and disciplined behavior."[21] Another report about the same area a couple of years later, by the resident CMS Superintendent, Miss K. E. Ritsert, gives further insight into the broad ethnic coverage of the student population in the Akabe school: "There are 54 boarders [sic] this year, 29 boys and 35 girls; these include children from Bida and Oworo, a few are Yoruba, 2 Igala, 1 Ijaw, and 1 Sierra Leone."[22] This has engendered a wide network of healthy relationships that have lasted many years, and even a lifetime with some blossoming into interreligious and intertribal marriages among the peoples of the Niger-Benue Confluence.

Impact of Missions on Social Institutions and Ceremonies

Many aspects of social institutions were reformed by the missionary encounter. Marriage, for instance, had its traditional procedure such as wooing, obligations from the family of the

21. Alvarez, "Lokoja-Bassa District," 2.

22. Ritsert, "Report of the Lokoja-Bassa District," 4. It is worth noting that the final tally of boarders in this quote reads 54 when it should actually be 64.

bride-groom-to-be toward the family of the bride-to-be, the bride-price (dowry), knowing the relations of the two families, and then the time when the bride is taken to the home of the groom. Lakpini describes the process among the Bassa Nges:

> After the traditional ceremonies have been completed, which may take seven days, the bride-to-be is finally led from the parents' or guardians' home to the home of the bridegroom-to-be with drumming, singing and dancing. Her property which may include some boxes, beds, beddings, earthenware and other expensive properties, depending on the wealth or status of her parents or guardians, will be carried to the bridegroom's house. The bride-to-be, who is now a real bride, is always accompanied by her bridesmaid and a number of her contemporary friends with one or two maid servants who are usually her younger sisters, cousins or near relations and who may live temporarily or permanently with her, depending on the circumstances obtaining.[23]

With the advent of Christianity some modifications were introduced, requiring that the parish priest be notified as well as the registry. Such notice is made public by way of banns of marriage announced on three consecutive Sundays, and a notice displayed in the registry in each case. The ceremony itself has an additional feature which is called the bachelor's eve and then the service of holy matrimony. While some have seen white weddings with suits and wedding gowns as the ideal Christian marriage, others have also accommodated the use of nativewear even for church weddings. There is usually the exchange of rings and the presentation of a white Bible which the bride picks as her most precious possession.[24]

What used to be the New Yam Festival in the communities was now Christianized and incorporated into the idea of harvest when farm produce was brought as a thank offering. The idea of rainmakers in times of drought had no attraction for the Christians

---

23. Lakpini, *History of Bassa (Nge)*, 118.
24. Pedraza, *Story of Lokoja*, 102.

anymore, for they believed God to be the One who controlled rainfall and bountiful harvest or drought.

The pattern of worship in the Anglican Church as introduced by the CMS was essentially intellectual. Literacy—however minimal—was necessary to an understanding of the Anglican liturgy. The hymns, the catechism, holy communion, baptism, wedding, morning and evening prayer—all were to be found in the *Book of Common Prayer* (BCP). The Holy Bible also had to be read. Even when there were translations, literacy was required to read the vernacular translations. All these factors made it incumbent on the converts to make an effort towards literacy. Of course, some who were too old to learn new ways memorized large portions of Scripture, and liturgy (especially the catechism, which was necessary for the rite of confirmation which admitted people to holy communion). They also memorized many hymns and special sections of the *Book of Common Prayer*, such as the Apostles' Creed, The Lord's Prayer, and the canticles (passages of the Bible sung during morning and evening prayers).

A rich versatility also developed as indigenous instruments and indigenous compositions were accommodated into worship services. In all these cases however, there was still a distinct difference between songs and instruments used for strictly cultural and traditional ceremonies and those used for Christian worship. There was both moderation in the rhythm, and clarity in their expression of Christian worship. For instance, as early as 1866, both Townsend and Crowther, on different occasions, had taken a favorable view on the native airs for which the church at Otta in the Yoruba Mission had become well known, describing their songs as "suitable Scriptural compositions of their own adapted to their native airs."[25] It is quite likely that the incorporation of local instruments into Christian worship was influenced by the emergence of the Independent African Church movement represented by the Babalola revival movement which attracted people to Ikare as earlier stated in this work. Lakpini who had been an eyewitness presents the experience in his own words:

25. Ade-Ajayi, *Christian Missions*, 225.

> In 1930, a new way of Christian evangelism came up in
> Ikare . . . when one Prophet Joseph Babalola from Odo-
> Owa, close to Iloffa and Omu-Aran . . . and also a staff
> of the Ministry of Works, was said to have seen a vision
> and began to spread the gospel of Christ, performing
> miracles publicly. By this incident, many Christian men
> and women, boys and girls, and even non-Christians,
> trooped from Bassa-Nge land, Lokoja, and environs to
> Ikare on foot. . . . My own evangelism came in, even
> though I was in school, when I had to lead or accompany
> my aunt . . . I became singularly conspicuous at Ikare be-
> cause I was the interpreter, dancing with the prophet and
> all his disciples on the large dais in the field at Ikare.[26]

The extent of the harmonious relationship between the religious adherents in the Niger-Benue Confluence area, especially
through the experience of missionary education became apparent.
Of course, the conclusions vary considerably where the element
of missionary education has been replaced with the takeover of
schools, which also led to the abolition of boarding facilities and
the teaching of Christian religious knowledge and Islamic religious
knowledge. The point being made is that missionary education laid
the foundation for a healthy interrelationship and a stable society.

Practices That Posed Serious Challenges

An undeniable fact, however, was the reality of evil in the community such as witchcraft, burying people alive on the understanding
that they were making servants to accompany their dead masters
to attend to them "through death, to the sacred realm beyond,"[27]
and similar practices which cut across the religious divides as an
ever-present threat from the supernatural world so that even some
of the church members were accused. By 1874, Crowther saw that
Christians, traditional religionists, and Muslims were becoming
quite a mixed group in some of these practices:

26. Lakpini, *History of Bassa (Nge)*, 172.
27. CMS, "Crowther to Venn," CA 3/04.

At Idah, for instance, it meant that Crowther had to look on helplessly as a respected elderly woman was accused by *Ata* Akaia, of witchcraft and forced to undergo the 'water of ordeal' (by poisoning) to determine whether she was innocent or guilty. Okoro, formerly slave to Akaia's grandfather, the *Ata* of Igala at the time of the Landers and McGregor Laird, was also accused of witchcraft, and, after the poison failed to work, was executed.[28]

The ever-present and widespread challenge of witchcraft continued to engage missionary attention as a factor that cannot be ignored anymore. Some explanations have been proffered:

> The spectacular growth of African Independent/Initiated Churches (AICs) in the early twentieth century is linked, in particular, to the inability of Western missions to come to terms with the reality of supernatural evil, especially witchcraft, and to articulate a Christian pastoral response to it.[29]

This phenomenon has raised a number of questions about the genuineness or depth of the conversions to Christianity. Even though missionary medical facilities were provided, there were cases that defied routine medical treatment and created fears in the minds of people in the communities. More and more it has become an accepted fact in missionary enterprise that most traditional religious settings had these expressions which the Christian faith could not afford to ignore. Indeed, biblical teaching has always pointed out these practices to be incompatible with the righteous lifestyle required by God:

> You shall not permit a sorceress to live. (Exod 22:18 NKJV)

> There shall not be found among you *anyone* who makes his son or his daughter pass through the fire, *or one* who practices witchcraft, *or* a soothsayer, or one who interprets omens, or a sorcerer. (Deut 18:10 NKJV)

28. McKenzie, *Inter-religious Encounters*, 61.

29. Asamoah-Gyadu, "Withcraft Accusations and Christianity in Africa," 1.

Missionary Impact on Family Life

A particularly radical, difficult, and controversial demand of missionary Christianity was the idea of monogamy. Polygamy was the widespread African practice that was not limited to the Niger-Benue Confluence area alone. It was a pillar of the African religious, socioeconomic worldview upon which so much hinged. With many wives, a man had many children. It was indeed an indication of a man's stature in society in a manner akin to the Old Testament picture that the man who had his quiver full of children was like a happy and unashamed warrior who stood shoulder-high to face his enemies in the gate (Ps 127:4–5).

In the traditional setting of the communities around the Niger-Benue Confluence, a man with many wives invariably had many sons, daughters, and sons-in-law, which translated to a workforce of considerable magnitude on the farms. Even though subsistence farming was in vogue, such large families could afford large hectares of farmland comparable to mechanized farming.

Polygamy was normative to traditional royal families as a sign of social prominence. In a mostly patrilineal setting, the man's responsibilities to his numerous wives were defined in favor of the man, while the wives each struggled to make ends meet for herself and her children while taking her queue in the schedule of chores, especially to ensure the satisfaction of the husband and the maintenance of the family.

Islam, which was the first foreign religion on the confluence, blended comfortably with polygamy up to a loosely defined, but never-compelled, limit of four wives. For this reason, Islam posed no threat to the social fabric of the indigenous communities. In his charge in 1866, Crowther put his thoughts down on polygamy:

> Many would place it prominently above all other obstacles in the way of Christian Missionaries in Africa; but perhaps I do not go to the same extent as they do in ranking it as the greatest hindrance in the way of the heathen embracing Christianity, though it is the most common.[30]

---

30. Crowther, *Charge Delivered on the Banks,* 25.

He provides a strong case—a sort of apologetics—rooted in the Bible, for the practice of monogamy. He then goes on to highlight the social difficulties in such a marriage as he admonished his people:

> Let us stand above the level, and take a view of this social evil. . . . When a man has commenced the life of a polygamist, he at the same time has commenced a life of neglect of conjugal duty and disquietude; the neglect creates quarrel, and disturbance of domestic peace ensues. It is impossible for every polygamist in this country to support from two to half a dozen wives out of his own scanty resources; and when this is the case, there is no alternative but that every wife must enter into a life of labor and drudgery . . . hence, to earn her livelihood, she must become a carrier of loads from one market town to another, or she must become a trader to neighboring towns and tribes, which involves an absence of days, and weeks, and months, from home; and on her return, it has not infrequently happened, that she provides for her husband out of her earnings, in addition to providing for herself and her children. . . . The occasional gift of a few cowries from the father to the children for their morning gruel, and perhaps occasional share of yams to the mother, constitute, mainly, the support from the father.[31]

It is on record that Crowther remained decidedly opposed to polygamists and would not baptize them, while his son Dandeson went even further by declaring polygamy to be "slavery for the wives."[32]

When missionary Christianity signaled monogamy as the biblical standard for their converts, those who fell short of the standard were barred from accessing the benefits of the sacraments of holy baptism and holy communion. While not all the converts could measure up to this standard, those who were engaged as native agents were required to comply. Indeed, the girls' hostels in Kpata and Akabe were more like convents and drew young girls

31. Crowther, *Charge Delivered on the Banks,* 29.
32. Ade-Ajayi, *Christian Missions,* 225.

from around the confluence communities and beyond (as in the case of Mrs. Comfort Ndagi, and even earlier, Mama Elizabeth Nmadu), from where the young bachelor teachers, evangelists, and catechists could find wives.

The Lambeth Conference of the Anglican Communion had tabled this matter for discussion from the earliest times. The first conference was in 1867, and by the third conference in 1888, the matter had received considerable attention as one requiring pastoral direction. At the said conference, it was resolved:

> That it is the opinion of this Conference that persons living in polygamy be not admitted to baptism, but may be accepted as candidates and kept under Christian instruction until such time as they shall be in a position to accept the law of Christ. That the wives of polygamists may, in the opinion of this Conference, be admitted in some cases to baptism, but that it must be left to the local authorities of the Church to decide under what circumstances they may be baptized.[33]

Subsequent conferences (1958, resolution 120; 1988, resolution 26; 2008, resolution 114) revisited the matter with considerable consistency of resolve, prohibiting polygamists from leadership positions, especially holy orders, and advising that the limitations placed on women should be remedied by the church by advancing their status in every way possible, especially in the sphere of education.

These conflicts, and the socioeconomic advantages of the extended family life notwithstanding, social change has vindicated the practice of monogamy as the best for a stable family life whereby each member pays special attention and takes responsibility for the other. Besides, the endless mutual suspicions, jealousy, squabbles over the sharing of real or imagined inheritance at the death of the head of the family, and other such crises—points which often fester in monogamous marriages—are greatly minimized. Quality education is ensured, and extended family members who are

---

33. Anglican Communion, "Lambeth Conference Resolutions Archive," Resolution 5.

afflicted by the vicissitudes of life are better assisted. The state of the family, being the smallest unit of the society, is a strong determinant of a healthy society where socialization is facilitated by more focused parenting that produces positive character traits in the younger generation that will become the future leaders. While monogamous marriage in itself cannot guarantee peace and stability, the Christian teaching about marriage and family life in the area of love and submission among couples, honor for parents, and moderation in the discipline of children, has ensured that, more than any other factor, the Christian missionary influence takes singular credit for this vital contribution at a critical point in life. While this has been an attraction to Christianity on the part of some, there are also those who have adopted this way of life while remaining Muslims, considering the advantages. It is to be admitted that most people in this category are among those who have been impacted by Western education and values as introduced by both the missionaries and the colonialists.

Conclusion

THE MISSIONARY ENTERPRISE
in RETROSPECT

IT IS RELEVANT AT THIS point to highlight the factors which this research shows to have been responsible for what has become the success story of the missionary enterprise in the Niger-Benue Confluence area.

The Nondiscriminatory Posture of the Pioneer Missionaries

The attitude of Samuel Ajayi Crowther and his workers toward the leadership of the Muslim community laid a solid foundation for religious harmony. They did not condemn Muslims they met, but rather engaged in respectable dialogue—including presenting Arabic Bibles to the traditional rulers to help them to gain a clearer perspective of the Christian faith they were introducing. In this way, even when the traditional rulers themselves did not make a commitment to the faith, they did not prevent their subjects from attending the schools or even converting to the new faith.

Religion Was Kept within Peaceful Boundaries

Religion was seen as an expression of personal choice, and a positive influence that was not allowed to be divisive, so long as it was not propagating ideas that were considered disruptive of the social structure. This is not to deny the instances of persecution that were encountered—the most widely recorded being that of Thomas Walter Bako, who was martyred at Tawari near Koton Karfe on 3rd June 1902 while returning from an evangelistic outing to develop new stations in the Koton Karfe and Umaisha areas, as mentioned earlier in this work. Even though his death was due to the attack of robbers rather than outright opposition to the Christian faith, it was nonetheless martyrdom.

It is noteworthy that his grandson, George Bako, became the pioneer bishop of the Diocese of Lokoja when it was created in October 1994. Furthermore, in the Lokoja community, another of his grandsons, Christopher A. S. H. Bako, was appointed a titleholder in the Lokoja traditional council.

Impact of Later Educational Policies

The takeover of mission schools in later decades by the Nigerian government, which at first appeared to be a harmless exercise, has turned out to be a major setback in the gains of missionary education and the congenial atmosphere it fostered for peaceful coexistence. Crowther Memorial College Lokoja (founded in 1964, in memory of Bishop Ajayi Crowther), and Bassa Nge Anglican Grammar School, Gboloko, (founded in 1969) as Anglican mission schools, were caught up in this turn of events and the implications have been disastrous. The story is not different with schools owned by the Roman Catholic Mission, such as the Bishop Delisle College (in memory of Augustine Delisle, Bishop of Kabba in 1964) in Lokoja. Prior to this development, many Muslim students could sing Christian hymns and recite Bible verses quite flawlessly. In the ensuing scenario, interaction was now limited to the classroom and the increasingly less structured field of sports. The teaching of

Christian religious knowledge, which did not compel conversion but exposed students from other faith backgrounds to the teaching of Christianity (indeed a good number of Muslim students performed better than their Christian counterparts in examinations), was gradually discontinued. First, it was the introduction of Islamic religious knowledge whereby students were separated according to their faith. The teaching of these religious studies have over the years been gradually phased out and replaced with civic education. This has been attributed, in government circles, to the increasing nonavailability of teachers in these subjects. Consequently, the boarding house facility which created a student community that encouraged healthy friendship beyond the classroom situation was discontinued. Students used the hours after school for mischief since the disciplined supervision and schedule of activities in the boarding school were now absent. Even hours of study became affected, resulting in poor grades and rampant cases of examination malpractices and teenage pregnancies. Some of the buildings that had been hostels or dormitories became abandoned and were not put to other uses, thereby becoming hideouts for hoodlums and sinister activities even among the students. While it is to be noted that the names of these schools have been retained, unlike the situation in some parts of the North whereby the names of mission schools have been replaced by indigenous heroes, miscreants who use the platform of religion to foment trouble always have to be watched.

Appendix 1

List of First Baptized Candidates in Gbobe and in Northern Nigeria

Given the paramount significance of baptism as an initiatory Christian rite, the list of those first fruits of the mission—the first baptized candidates as found in Ajayi Crowther's records—is worth reproducing here, showing the family connection of some of them, and their respective tribes:

1. Abraham Ayikuta: a nephew of King AMA Abokko was at Idda about the month of June, 1860 when he first heard of the proceedings of the Society's Scripture Reading at Gbebe, from that time he removed from Idda and took his abode here, joined the class of Candidates for baptism, cast away all his idols, refused to do any more superstitious customs, dismissed his superfluous wife, and being a firm candidate, though he suffered much from his father Amadako, who tried to bring him back to idolatry, on the 14th of September he was baptized by the name of Abraham.

2. Eve Embi: an elderly widow and granddaughter of one of the Atas of Igara, was born and brought up a heathen, and was also a long time with the Mohammedans in the Hausa country, but she found that Christianity was more suited to

her case as a sinner than either of the above religions, joined the class of candidates with her son and daughter, and was baptized by the name of Eve.

3. John Kpanaki: the son of Eve Embi and great grandson of one of the Atas of Igara joined the class of candidates with his mother and sister at Gbebe; on one occasion, he was one of a party in a canoe to Idda market; when their articles were not soon sold, a proposal was made by the headman of the canoe to collect cowries to consult and propitiate the gods to make their trade prosperous, in which John Kpanaki refused to join, being conscious of its foolishness. Consequently he was turned out of the canoe at Idda, but fortunately for him, his articles were soon bought up in the presence of his superstitious companions, so he took passage in another canoe and returned to Gbebe and made a total clearance of his gods. Being a constant candidate, he was baptized by the name of John.

4. Susannah Ada: a young daughter of Eve Embi has made up her mind to cast in her lot with the mother and brother in the profession of the Christian religion; she has kept very close to our church and class of candidates since the last two years and was baptized by the name of Susannah. The above four persons are of mixed blood of Igarra and Igbira.

5. Maria Ayin: of the Eki or Bunu tribe, Maria was the first that joined the class of candidates at this place, never missed church or class unless prevented by sickness, which was very seldom; she being an old slave of the first wife of King Ama was reserving cowries for her own ransom, which has been affected by my indisposition since last year; showing her faith in Christ as her all sufficient Savior, she was baptized by the name of Maria.

6. Phebe Amoye: also of the Ekie tribe, Phebe was a companion of Ayin, joined class with her about the same time, was a regular attendant on the means of grace since 1858, was baptized at the same time with Ayin.

7. Fanny Aniki: a widow (of late Ayo, who also was a candidate for baptism when he died two years ago, both of the Eki tribe) remaining a regular attendant on the means of grace and looking only to Jesus for salvation and to no other, she was baptized by the name of Fanny.

8. Sarah Olojo: of the Ekie tribe, Sarah is a very quiet and unassuming person, though her husband is a very superstitious priest of Ifa, yet, she joined the class of candidates, against which her husband put no hindrance on her way, but seemed rather to encourage it, having renounced all idolatory and made up her mind to walk according to the precepts of the Christian religion, she was baptized by the name of Sarah. The above four persons are of the Ekie or Bunu tribe.

9. Hannah Asetu: an aged woman of the Yoruba tribe who was formerly a slave to a Nupe by whom she was brought to this place; she has since obtained her freedom; she was very superstitious, but being frequently visited and spoken to by the Scripture Readers, she at last cast away her gods and joined the class of candidates, though she is too old to learn much, but as she believed that her only hope of salvation is in Jesus Christ, so she was baptized by the name of Hannah.

10. Lydia Lami: a Gbari woman, formerly a slave to a Mohammedans family; she attended our service since 1859, from which time there was some disagreement between her and her master and mistress; they determined to sell her to the Abo people though on the eve of becoming a mother. On application to me she was relieved from her troubles by a loan of five bags of cowries which she promised to labor for and pay; she was baptized by the name of Lydia. Her infant son a fine child which was born in the mission yard shortly after her removal thither after her ransom, being a child of about 11 months old, was baptized with her by the name of John Venn.[1]

---

1. Crowther, "List of Baptized Candidates," CA3/04/118.

Bibliography

Ade-Ajayi, Jacob F. *Christian Missions in Nigeria 1841–1891: The Making of a New Elite*. Evanston, IL: Northwestern University Press, 1965.

———. "From Mission to Church: The Heritage of the Church Missionary Society." In *The Anglican Church in Nigeria, 1842–1992*, edited by Akinyele Omoyajowo, xxvi–xliii. Lagos: Macmillan Nigeria, 1994.

———. *A Patriot to the Core: Bishop Ajayi Crowther*. Ibadan, Nigeria: Spectrum, 2001.

Adebiyi, Peter. *History of Christianity in Ekitiland (1893-1973)*, Lagos: CSS, 1973.

African Church Centenary Committee. *The History of the African Church, (October 13, 1901 October 13, 2001)*. Lagos: The African Church National Secretariat, 2002.

Aitken, J. D. "The Mission Field." *Church Missionary Intelligencer* 27 (August 1902) 610–12.

Ajala, Theophilus A., & , Peter A. Ajagbe. *First Baptist Church, Lokoja at 100 Years 1913-2013*. Oyo, Nigeria: Odumatt, 2013.

Ajayi, Olaseinde W. "A History of the Niger and Northern Nigeria Missions, 1857–1914." Unpublished PhD Diss., submitted to the University of Bristol, 1963.

Akamisoko, Duke. *Samuel Ajayi Crowther in the Lokoja Area*. Ibadan, Nigeria: Sefer, 2002.

Allen, Roland. *Missionary Methods: St Paul's or Ours?* Grand Rapids: Eerdmans, 1962.

Alokan, Adeware. *The Christ Apostolic Church, C.A.C. 1928–1988*. Ibadan, Nigeria: Ibukunola, 1991.

Alvarez, Thomas. "Report of the Lokoja-Bassa District, March 15-Nov. 25, 1937" CMS Memo, AF 35/49 G3 A9 G6.

Amihere, K. Micah. *History of the Cathedral Church of The Holy Trinity, Lokoja*. Lagos: CSS, 2004.

Anglican Communion. "Lambeth Conference Resolutions Archive." https://www.anglicancommunion.org/media/127722/1888.pdf.

Anglican Diocese of Kaduna History Committee. *A History of the Diocese of Kaduna (Anglican Communion).* Wusasa-Zaria, Nigeria: Tamaza, 2004.

Asamoah-Gyadu, K. J. "Witchcraft Accusations and Christianity in Africa." *International Bulletin of Missionary Research* 39.1 (2015) 23–27.

Ayandele, A. Emmanuel. *African Historical Studies.* London: Routledge, 1979.

———."The Missionary Factor in Northern Nigeria, 1870–1918." *Journal of the Historical Society of Nigeria* 3.3 (1966) 503–22.

———. *The Missionary Impact on Modern Nigeria 1842–1914: A Political and Social Analysis.* London: Longmans, 1966.

Babalola, Emmanuel O. *Christianity in West Africa (The Historical Analysis).* Ibadan, Nigeria: Scholar, 1967.

Baikie, Adamu. *Against All Odds: An Autobiography.* Wusasa-Zaria: Tamaza, 2011.

Baikie, William B. *Narrative of an Exploring Voyage Up the Rivers Kwora and Binue Commonly Known as the Niger and Tsadda in 1854.* London: John Murray, 1856.

Bane, Martin J. *Catholic Pioneers in West Africa.* Dublin: Clonmore and Reynolds, 1956.

Barnes, Andrew E. *Making Headway: The Introduction of Western Civilization in Colonial Northern Nigeria.* Rochester, NY: University of Rochester, 2009.

Bello, U. M. "The Growth and Development of the Missionary Activities and Their Impact on Lokoja in the 20th Century: A Historical Perspective." Unpublished dissertation submitted to the Department of History of the University of Sokoto, for Bachelor of Arts Degree in History, 1988.

Bowen, Thomas J. *Adventures and Missionary Labours in Several Countries in the Interior of Africa from 1849 to 1856.* 2nd edition. London: Cass, 1968.

Buxton, Fowell T. *The African Slave Trade and Its Remedy.* London: John Murray, 1840.

CA3/04/118; List of baptized Candidates at Gbebe–1862.

CA2/056 J. Johnson to Hutchinson, 6 March 1876.

Church Missionary Intelligencer, 1866, 1849-1906.

Church Missionary Intelligencer, January 1880.

Church Missionary Intelligencer (March 1890). Vol. XV New Series. London: Gilbert and Rivington, 1890.

Church Missionary Society. "The Missionary Supervisor of Schools." Notes Upon the Work, as in the Niger Mission, by the Rev J. M. Carr. January 1937.

Church Missionary House. "Missionary Education in The Niger Diocese." April 22, 1930.

CMS. "Crowther to Venn, 9/11/1863." CA3/04.

CMS Northern Nigeria Executive Committee. Feb. 1909, 1932.

Crampton, Edmund P. T. *Christianity in Northern Nigeria.* London: Chapman, 1979.

———. *Christianity in Northern Nigeria.* With update by Professor Musa A. B. Gaiya. Jos, Nigeria: ACTS, 2004.

Crowder, Michael. *The Story of Nigeria*. London: Faber and Faber, 1962.

Crowther, Samuel A. *A Charge Delivered on the Banks of the River Niger in West Africa*. London: Seeley, Jackson, & Halliday, 1866.

———. *Report of the Overland Journey from Lokoja to Bida, on the River Niger, and Thence to Lagos, on the Seacoast, from November 10th, 1871 to February 8th, 1872*. London: Seeley, Jackson & Halliday, 1872.

Davies, Madeleine. "Canterbury Remembers Crowther." *Church Times*, July 4, 2014. https://www.churchtimes.co.uk/articles/2014/4-july/news/uk/canterbury-remembers-crowther.

Décorvet, Jeanne, and Oladipo, Emmanuel. *Samuel Ajayi Crowther: The Miracle of Grace*. Lagos: CSS, 2006.

Dike, Onwuka K. *Origins of the Niger Mission, 1841–1891*. Ibadan, Nigeria: Ibadan University Press, 1957.

Dobinson, H. "Letter to Baylis, CMS Secretary." 30 March, 1896. G3A3/1896/54.

Donovan, Vincent J. *Christianity Rediscovered*. New York: Orbis, 1982.

Egbunu, Emmanuel, A. S. "Assessing Colonial Involvement." In *Issues and Trends in the Growth and Development of Christianity: Essays in Honour of Professor G. O. M. TASIE, FNAL, KSC, OFR;*, edited by Cyril O. Imo et al., 1–19. Kaduna, Nigeria: Baraka, 2020.

———. "Racial Tension in Mission: Reviewing the Niger Mission Crisis (1875–97) and Its Implications for Mission." *Anvil* 36.3 (2020) 19–25.

Ekechi, Felix K. *Missionary Enterprise and Rivalry in Igboland, 1857–1914*. London: Cass, 1972.

Epelle, Sam. *The Promise of Nigeria*. New Mills, UK: Pan, 1960.

Ezebube, Chukwurah. *George Bako, Bishop of Lokoja, The Controversial Fool for Christ*. Lagos: CSS, 2000.

Falola, Toyin, ed. *Tradition and Change in Africa: The Essays of J. F. Ade-Ajayi*. Trenton, NJ: Africa World, 2000.

Fatusi, Olayemi T. "The Retransmission of Evangelical Christianity in Nigeria: The Legacy and Lessons from Bishop Samuel Ajayi Crowther's Life and Ministry (1810–1891)." *Southwestern Journal of Theology* 61.2 (Spring 2019) 153–65.

Fretheim, Sara J. *Kwame Bediako and African Christian Scholarship*. Eugene, OR: Pickwick, 2018.

G3A3/04 "Letter from a friend to the Rev. A.C. Strong at Brass" marked "Confidential."

G3A3/1896/54. Dobinson, H. H. to Baylis, 30 March 1896.

Grimley, John B., and Gordon E. Robinson. *Church Growth in Central and Southern Nigeria*. Grand Rapids, Eerdmans, 1966.

Hamilton, James. "West Africa." *The Church Missionary Gleaner* 14 (1887) 4.

Harford-Battersby, Charles F. *The Keswick Convention: Its Message, Its Method and Its Men*. London: Paternoster, 1907.

Hewitt, Gordon E. *The Problems of Success: A History of the Church Missionary Society, 1910–1942*. Vol. 1. 2 vols. London: SCM, 1971.

Higgins, James. "History of the Church in Mid-West Nigeria, Society of African Missions." http://www.sma.ie/africa-module/45-sma-in-africa.

Hodgkin, Thomas. *Nationalism in Colonial Africa*. New York: New York University Press, 1952.

Hooper, Handley D. CMS: "The Present Crisis and Future Policy" Educational Work in African Missions. July 12, 1926.

Isichei, Elizabeth. "Does Christianity Empower Women? The Case of the Anaguta of Central Nigeria." In *Women and Missions: Past and Present: Anthropological and Historical Perceptions,* edited by Fiona Bowie et al, 209–27. London: Routledge, 1993.

———. *A History of Christianity in Africa: From Antiquity to the Present.* Grand Rapids: Eerdmans, 1995.

———. *Varieties of Christian Experience in Nigeria.* London, Macmillan, 1982.

Jenkins, Philip. *The Next Christendom: The Coming of Global Christianity.* New York: Oxford University Press, 2011.

Johnson, Akinpelu B. C. *As For Me and My House...The Story of a Levitical Dynasty.* Lagos: Wellsprings, 2007.

Kolapo, Femi J. *Christian Missionary Engagement in Central Nigeria, 1857–1891: The Church Missionary Society's All-African Mission on the Upper Niger.* Cham, Switzerland: Palgrave Macmillan, 2019.

———. "Christian Missions and Religious Encounters at the Niger-Benue Confluence." In *Precolonial Nigeria: Essays in Honor of Toyin Falola,* edited by Akinwumi Ogundiran, 509–24. Trenton, NJ: Africa World, 2005.

———. "The CMS and the Failure of Christian Transition in Middle Nigeria." A presentation at the 19th International Biennial Conference of The African Studies Association. Hanover, Germany, June 2–5, 2004.

———. "CMS Missionaries of African Origin and Extra-Religious Encounters at the Niger-Benue Confluence, 1858–1880." *African Studies Review* 43.2 (2000) 87–115.

———. *The Gbebe and Lokoja Journals of James Thomas, C.M.S Missionary, Pioneer Teacher and Pastor, 1858–1879,* Guelph, ON: University of Guelph Press, 2009.

———. "The Gbebe Journals of James Ikubaje Thomas." *African Studies Review* 43.2 (2000) 87–115.

Lakpini, Christopher A. M. *History of Bassa (Nge) Ethnic Group of Nupe Origin and The Autobiography of Pa Chief Christopher Amos Mawo Lakpini, CHM.* Lagos: CSS, 2004.

"Lokoja-Bassa District Report, Oct. 1st 1938–Mar 20th 1939." CMS Archives, 34/9. Cadbury Research Library. Birmingham, UK.

Lugard, Frederick D. (1915). "Mission Schools in the Northern Provinces, Report on Progress During the Year 1915." SNP 8, 87/1917.

Makozi, A. O., and Ojo Afolabi. *The History of the Catholic Church in Nigeria.* Lagos: Macmillan Nigeria, 1982.

McKenzie, P. R. *Inter-religious Encounters in West Africa: Samuel Ajayi Crowther's Attitude to African Traditional Religion and Islam*. Leicester, UK: University of Leicester Press, 1976.

Miller, W. R. S. *Reflections of a Pioneer*. Church Missionary Society, London, 1936.

Murray, Victor. "Statement of Missionary Education Policy Discussed at the Meeting of the Christian Council of Nigeria, April 1–2, 1932," in Lagos, Nigeria, April 1–2, 1932. https://doi.org/10.1111/j.1758-6631.1932.tb04509.x.

Oldham, Joseph H. "CMS General Secretary to Oldham." 18th December 1930.

Omolewa, Michael. *Nigeria Through the Eyes of Lokoja*. Lokoja, Nigeria: Goke International, 2014.

Omoyajowo, Akin. "The Aladura Churches in Nigeria since Independence." In *Christianity in Independent Africa*, edited by Edward Fashole-Luke et al., 96–110. London: Rex Collings, 1978.

Our Saviour's Church, TBS, Lagos. *From Colonial to Cosmopolitan: The Story of Our Saviour's Church, Tafawa Balewa Square, Lagos (1911–2011)*. Lagos: Our Saviour's Church, TBS, 2015.

Page, Jesse. *The Black Bishop, Samuel Ajayi Crowther*. Chicago: Fleming, 1910.

Page, Jesse, and Samuel Crowther. *The Slave Boy Who Became Bishop of the Niger*. Project Canterbury. London: Partridge, 1892.

Pedraza, Howard J. *Borrioboola-Gha: The Story of Lokoja, the First British Settlement in Nigeria*. London: Oxford University Press, 1960.

Peel, John D. Y. *Aladura: A Religious Movement among the Yoruba*. London: Oxford University Press, 1968.

Peter, Kazenga T. "The Beginnings of Girls' Education in the Native Administration Schools in Northern Nigeria, 1930–1945." *The Journal of African History* 26 (1985) 93–109.

Porter, Andrew N. "Cambridge, Keswick, and Late-Nineteenth-Century Attitudes to Africa." *The Journal of Imperial and Commonwealth History* 5.1 (1976) 5–34.

———. "'Cultural Imperialism' and Protestant Missionary Enterprise, 1788–1914." *The Journal of Imperial and Commonwealth History* 25.3 (1997) 367–91.

Rae, R. E. V. "Arrest of C.M.S. Evangelists." No 95/1928/33 in *Complaints by and against Christian Converts and Missionaries; Provincial Correspondence*, NAK Jacket 95/1928.

Ritsert, Katerine E., "Report of the Lokoja-Bassa District." March 1943, CMS AF 35/49 G3 A9 G6.

Robinson, Gordon E. *Church Growth in Central and Southern Nigeria*. Grand Rapids: Eerdmans, 1966.

Rose, Susan (ed.), *The Naval Miscellany, Vol. VII*, The Navy Records Society, Ashgate Publishing, Hants, England, 2008.

Sanneh, Lamin. "The CMS and the African Transformation: Samuel Ajayi Crowther and the Opening of Nigeria." In *The Church Mission Society and*

World Christianity, 1799–1999, edited by Kevin Ward and Brian Stanley, 173–97. Grand Rapids: Eerdmans, 2000.

———. *West African Christianity: The Religious Impact.* New York: Orbis, 1993.

———. *Whose Religion Is Christianity? The Gospel beyond the West,* Grand Rapids: Eerdmans, 2003.

Shenk, Wilbert. *Henry Venn—Missionary Statesman.* Eugene, OR: Wipf and Stock, 2006.

Smith, Alfred. Letter dated 3rd February 1932, in *Complaints by and against Christian Converts and Missionaries; Provincial Correspondence,* NAK Jacket 95/1928.

Stock, Eugene. *The History of the Church Missionary Society: Its Environment, Its Men, and Its Work.* 4 vols. London: CMS, 1899.

Strobel, Margaret. *European Women and the Second British Empire.* Bloomington: Indiana University Press, 1991.

Sturdy, Gareth. "Do Not Despise the Day of Small Things." *Yes Magazine* (May-August 2007) 7–13.

Suleiman, Muhammad D. *The Hausa in Lokoja, 1860–1966; A Study of the Evolution of a Migrant Community in the Niger-Benue Confluence.* Zaria, Nigeria: Gaskiya, 2001.

Sundkler, Bengt G. M. *Bantu Prophets in Africa.* Cambridge: Clarke, 2004.

Tasie, Godwin. *Christian Missionary Enterprise in the Niger Delta 1864–1918,* Leiden: Brill, 1978.

———. "The Vernacular Church and Nigerian Christianity." Inaugural Lecture, University of Jos, July 2, 1997.

Taylor, William D. "Greatest Personal Lessons from Serving Seventeen Years in Latin America." *Evangelical Missions Quarterly* 39.3 (2003) 316–17.

Thomas, E. A. J. "Preaching Christ on the Upper Niger." *Church Missionary Intelligencer* 23 (August 1898) 584–87.

Townsend, Henry. Journal for June 1857; CMS CA2/085.

Turaki, Yusufu. *Theory and Practice of Christian Missions in Africa: A Century of SIM/ECWA History and Legacy in Nigeria, 1893–1993, Volume One.* Nairobi: International Bible Society Africa, 1999.

Uruakpa, Joseph A. "The Anglican Church and Educational Development in The Eastern States of Nigeria 1857–1966." In *The Niger Mission: Origin, Growth and Impact 1857–1995,* edited by Shed Adiele, 123–41. Aba, Nigeria: Isaeco, 1996.

Walls, Andrew. *The Cross-Cultural Process in Christian History.* New York: Orbis, 2004.

———. *The Missionary Movement in Christian History: Studies in the Transmission of Faith.* New York: Orbis, 2001.

Wilkinson, E. F. CMS Memo on "The Missionary Supervisor of Schools: Notes upon the Work in the Niger Mission." 1936.

www.ingramcontent.com/pod-product-compliance
Lightning Source LLC
Chambersburg PA
CBHW071130280326
41935CB00010B/1169